# The French Foreign Legion

# The French Foreign Legion

David King's
*Ten Thousand Shall Fall*

Edited and introduced by
Paul Rich

WESTPHALIA PRESS
An imprint of Policy Studies Organization

**The French Foreign Legion:**
**David King's *Ten Thousand Shall Fall***

All Rights Reserved © 2013 by Policy Studies Organization

Westphalia Press
An imprint of Policy Studies Organization
dgutierrezs@ipsonet.org

*All rights reserved.* No part of this book may be reproduced or transmitted in any form or by any means graphic, electronic, or mechanical, including photocopying, recording, taping, or by any information storage or retrieval system, without the permission in writing from the publisher.

For information:
Westphalia Press
1527 New Hampshire Ave., N.W.
Washington, D.C. 20036

ISBN-13: 978-0944285879
ISBN-10: 0944285872

Updated material and comments on this edition can be found at the Policy Studies Organization website:
http://www.ipsonet.

This edition is dedicated to Dermot McMahon, remembering our days in Riyadh.

# Also from Westphalia Press
westphaliapress.org

*The Idea of the Digital University*

*Masonic Tombstones and Masonic Secrets*

*Treasures of London*

*The History of Photography*

*L'Enfant and the Freemasons*

*Baronial Bedrooms*

*Making Trouble for Muslims*

*Material History and Ritual Objects*

*Paddle Your Own Canoe*

*Opportunity and Horatio Alger*

*Careers in the Face of Challenge*

*Bookplates of the Kings*

*Collecting American Presidential Autographs*

*Freemasonry in Old Buffalo*

*Original Cables from the Pearl Harbor Attack*

*Social Satire and the Modern Novel*

*The Essence of Harvard*

*The Genius of Freemasonry*

*A Definitive Commentary on Bookplates*

*James Martineau and Rebuilding Theology*

*No Bird Lacks Feathers*

*Earthworms, Horses, and Living Things*

*The Man Who Killed President Garfield*

*Anti-Masonry and the Murder of Morgan*

*Understanding Art*

*Homeopathy*

*Ancient Masonic Mysteries*

*Collecting Old Books*

*Masonic Secret Signs and Passwords*

*The Thomas Starr King Dispute*

*Earl Warren's Masonic Lodge*

*Lariats and Lassos*

*Mr. Garfield of Ohio*

*The Wisdom of Thomas Starr King*

*War in Syria*

*Naturism Comes to the United States*

*New Sources on Women and Freemasonry*

*Designing, Adapting, Strategizing in Online Education*

*Policy Diagnosis*

*Meeting Minutes of Naval Lodge No. 4 F.A.A.M.*

*Shells Crash And Whine:*

PREFACE TO THE NEW EDITION

IN John Bowe's *Soldiers of the Legion* (Peterson, Chicago, 1918), he describes David King: "Providence, R.I., member of a family connected with cement products interests in England and America, a Harvard graduate—of uncomplaining and unflinching disposition, though small in stature, he was great in courage. I have seen him marching without a whimper when his feet were so sore that only the toes of one foot could touch the ground. He always had an extra cake or two of chocolate, and was willing to divide with the individual who could furnish fire or water. He changed from the Foreign Legion to the 170th, in 1915, and was seriously wounded in 1916. On recovery he went into the Artillery."

King enlisted in the Legion in August 1914. He was awarded the Croix de Guerre for heroism. He resigned in November 1917 to accept a commission in the United States Army and was appointed assistant military attaché at the American Legation in Berne, Switzerland. He returned after to Paris to write a novel, but Irving Werstein remarks, "Actually, he spent more time at cafe sidewalk tables drinking Pernod than he did at his desk, writing." (Crowell, New York, 1967.) Nevertheless, King's account of the Legion remains a fascinating insight into one of the most storied of all military units.

              Paul Rich

*Ten Thousand Shall Fall*

*"A thousand shall fall at thy side, and ten thousand at thy right hand; but it shall not come nigh thee."*

**The Ninety-first Psalm of David**

*Sniping from the church. Craonnelle.*

# TEN THOUSAND
# SHALL FALL

By
Soldier 8046 of The Foreign Legion
DAVID KING

With an Introduction by
HENDRIK WILLEM VAN LOON

Duffield & Company
MCMXXX

*Copyright, 1927, by*
*Duffield & Company*
*Printed in the United States of America*
*By The Cornwall Press, Inc.*

*To the gamest man
I know,—the Lemon.*

# FOREWORD

*It was in the year . . . . . to tell you the truth I don't exactly remember the year . . . . . but it was in that strange era before the war . . . . . when all the problems of the human race had been settled for good and all . . . . . when the millenium was merely a question of time . . . . . it was in that vague prehistoric period of our middle-aged selves before the year of grace 1914 . . . . . that I paid my last visit to Cambridge.*

*I don't remember exactly why I should have returned to the banks of the Charles River, but in those days (if my memory serves me right) there were a few well-intentioned people who thought that I ought to teach History and they made discreet arrangements with certain College Authorities (for whom I had a wholesome respect) to let me give a few lectures on my own*

## FOREWORD

chosen subjects and show what *I* could do and to see what could be done with me.

And it was, *I* think, during one of those futile expeditions into a hostile territory that *Lin Neale*, most faithful of friends, told me that he knew some sort of an infant in the *Harvard* freshman class and that whenever *I* got tired of being on my good behavior (which happened with astonishing and most regrettable celerity) *I* ought to call on this child and refresh my sagging spirits.

And *I* remember that *I* climbed many stairs of a dormitory somewhere near or on the *Gold Coast* and that *I* met a pleasant youngster (thirty-five talking to twenty-one) and that we tumbled at once into an incredibly rapid and vulgar jargon of *French* and *American* . . . . . that we went to strange culinary establishments (it was before the days of the hygienic cafeterias, when ham-and-eggs was ham-and-eggs and not a combination of calories and hormones) . . . . . and that whenever the conversation lagged we listened to the wails of those *Hawaiian* guitars which were then conquering the country by storm.

*Whereupon I departed* (having been weighed

## FOREWORD

*and found wanting) and floundered for years through the dismal swamps of failure and disappointment and then someone in a distant land shot an inconsequential Hapsburg grandee and this fine pretty world came to an end and some of us were blown to shreds and the others were blown to the four corners of the compass and the curtain descended upon the final act of our youth.*

*How and when and where and under what circumstances I met young King again I really could not tell. I have a hazy recollection that his brother one day swore loudly and eloquently and said, "Look what that damn-fool kid has done now," and showed me a cable which read, "The joke is on you. I enlisted and am in the Foreign Legion."*

*Then silence until it was all over and seventeen million people (white, brown, red and intermediary shades) lay dead and buried and the rest of us returned from our different tasks to pick up the odds and ends of existence and try and shape ourselves some sort of tolerable future amidst the ruins of our glories and our hopes.*

*When I saw King again he sported the remnants of a uniform, he coughed distressingly,*

## FOREWORD

*he hobbled slightly, and was no longer a creature of flesh and blood but one composed of the usual ingredients plus a considerable quantity of platinum and silver. Furthermore he grinned as if he had just lived through a very ghastly joke and talked a French dialect which was as utterly beyond my reach as if it had been a combination of Hindustani and Finnish. By and by a few English phrases filtered through his torrent of words and then I began to understand that he had not only served in the Foreign Legion but had actually survived the experience and was willing and even eager to let me know what he had seen and done and thought.*

*But this was no easy task for he resembled a man who has spent himself in a race. He had reached his goal but he was too much out of breath, too miserably exhausted to do anything but gasp and beat the air and say "oof."*

*And so we looked at each other, smiled sheepishly and let it go at that. Until after nine years of restless wandering, of endless trekking from place to place, he caught up with whatever was left of the procession and did a wise thing.*

*He rid his memory of its ghastly burden and wrote a book.*

# FOREWORD

*I am glad that he did and I am even more glad that he did it the way he did it because we are sorely in need of just such honest scraps of downright and fearless documentation.*

*To tell you the truth, I detest war. In the first place I am dreadfully scared whenever people begin to fire off guns and throw bombs. In the second place, I have spent my life among the events of the past and I can see no earthly good in almost any war except that it affords a Roman Holiday to the more sadistically inclined among our females and gives a large number of our male neighbors a chance to escape from the uncomfortable bondage of modern civilization and for once in their career do the things they would like to do if they had been given their choice.*

*At the same time I fully realize the futility of fighting the idea of "war" by mere oratory and moral precept.*

*The brass bands are all on the other side and what chance has a shabby prophet against a lieutenant-colonel in full dress uniform?*

*But books, my friends, those little books writ by the poor devils who did the dirty work, they are a different matter.*

# FOREWORD

*They had a hard time coming into their own. Who wanted to read what the common soldiers had to say when the Honorable Statesmen had just condescended to explain their blunders and to favor us with their alibis?*

*For a long time the answer was "no one."*

*But a change is coming over us.*

*The incredible is happening.*

*The cannon-fodder of yester-war is just becoming articulate. The Unknown Soldier is endeavoring to explain why he lies beneath a heavy slab of granite instead of disporting himself with his kids among the blood-red poppies which looked so lovely in the dear poems about the Flemish slaughter-house.*

*This book of David King's is not a sermon.*

*It does not preach and it carries no moral.*

*It says in fact: "Here, my good friends who made me into a beautiful hero, is what happened to me while I was gaining that title. Take it or leave it and be damned to you or have a drink with me or do whatever you please, but for Heaven's sake don't kiss me for I am splashed with the blood of my dead comrades and I am dirty with the grime of a million miles of road."*

*It says all this without any rancour, without*

## FOREWORD

*any show of ill-feeling, patiently and a little pityingly for those who remained at home and sold ribbons for war medals and saved prune-stones for gas-masks.*

*May the Lord in his mercy deprive them temporarily of a sense of shame. Amen.*

## CONTENTS

| CHAPTER | | PAGE |
|---|---|---|
| I. | WAR FEVER | 3 |
| II. | MOVING UP AND SHAKING DOWN | 22 |
| III. | IN FOR KEEPS | 38 |
| IV. | A CUP OF COFFEE AND A RIOT | 52 |
| V. | SCRAPS | 64 |
| VI. | BATTLE OF CHAMPAGNE | 76 |
| VII. | WE LEAVE AND RELIEVE THE LEGION | 95 |
| VIII. | VERDUN—SHOCK TROOPS | 102 |
| IX. | VERDUN AGAIN—AND SPRING | 127 |
| X. | BATTLE OF THE SOMME | 137 |
| XI. | I CHANGE ARMS—THEN ARMIES | 149 |
| XII. | . . . . AND PEACE? | 172 |

# ILLUSTRATIONS

Sniping from the church, Craonnelle . *Frontispiece*

*Facing Page*

Legion material,—August, 1914 . . . . . . 6

A month later . . . . . . . . . . . 7

My partner in the laundry business . . . . 32

Alan Seeger, Boligni, Nielsen, Morlac,—Little Chateau, Craonnelle . . . . . . . . 54

Alan Seeger, Street of Craonnelle, November, '14   55

Conti,—Dog Fancier . . . . . . . . . 66

The Legion on the March, August, '15 . . . 67

"Shirt reading" between attacks, Champagne, September, 1916 . . . . . . . . . 86

"And some dig deeper in the chalk" . . . . . 87

One of a million . . . . . . . . . . . 98

"A little home cooking,"—Hoffeber, Dugan, Rocle, Gans (all killed) . . . . . . . 99

## ILLUSTRATIONS

The redoubt of Vaux, Verdun, March 1st, 1916  114
Verdun, April, 1916 . . . . . . . . . . 115
The second Company continues to advance . . 142
Into the first German line, Somme, 1916 . . . 143
Where did that one go? . . . . . . . . . 164
Going over the top, Somme, August, 1916 . . . 165

*Ten Thousand Shall Fall*

*Chapter One*

## WAR FEVER

"TAKE off those socks!"

My turn. No chance of deception, as flat feet were a grave defect in the early days of the war, when men were still plentiful.

Name. Age. Nationality. Stethoscope. Open your mouth. Weight. Height. ... A few prods and I was in. *"Bon pour lc service."*

Not very convincing, that scribble on a bit of paper with some sort of government stamp on one corner. The little clerk in uniform seemed satisfied, however, and scribbled away like mad after every question. The cigarette, stuck to the left side of his lower lip seemed a permanent part of him, but as I looked, it suddenly appeared on the right side, though both hands were busily engaged with the papers. It shifted again, and this time I discovered, with awe and admiration, that he could roll it from one side of his face to the other.

I produced another cigarette which the scribe filed for future reference behind his left ear, and asked him a few questions.

"What regiment will they assign me to?"

"Can you ride?"

"Yes."

"Probably the Dragoons or Hussars then."

Good news. That meant active service and no danger of being stuck guarding railroad bridges miles from the front.

"Here you are. 9:10 A. M. tomorrow. Rouen. Gare St. Lazare. And report at the barracks of the 135th when you get there."

A hurried breakfast with two Hollanders I had picked up the day before, then by fighting, kicking, struggling, and the aid of a sergeant major, we gained the privilege of standing in a compartment with sixteen others.

At Rouen we arrived at the barracks just in time to see the regiment, the 135th, march out to entrain. Fascinating scene—company after company filing out of the barracks-building into the square; adjutants and sergeant majors running from section to section checking up

## WAR FEVER

equipment and emergency rations, officers standing around the colonel receiving final instructions, and the feeling of excited orderly confusion run riot through twenty-five hundred men tuned up to war pitch. A sudden sharp order and the confusion ceased. The lines stiffened into solid blocks of red and blue. Another order, drums began to roll. The blocks broke up into columns and swayed out of the barrack gates. The brazen blare of bugles swelled the rumble of the drums as they moved down the street, the glorious music rising and falling till only the distant rhythm of the drums could be heard. Last the clink of equipments and the steady soft swishing of hundreds of feet in step.

We found the volunteers quartered in what had been a school for young ladies. An Arab in Spahis uniform stopped us at the gate, till we produced our orders from the recruiting office. We passed into the court and into the Army.

The place was crowded but I found a bale of compressed fodder and camped down on it, fully convinced that I was already experiencing the hardships of war. I fell asleep listening to a couple of King's hard bargains discussing the possibility of drawing two uniforms each and selling one.

Five o'clock the next morning and everything stir and confusion. *"Deux hommes de bonne volontée!"* My imagination ran wild. Perhaps the Germans were advancing on Rouen! It might mean lighting the fuse to blow up the bridge, or a forlorn hope, and seeing myself the last man in a desperate rear-guard action, I sprang forward to volunteer. Another American followed and the sergeant led us off.

Disillusionment was ours. He handed us each a mop and bucket, and planted us before a row of filthy latrines. "Report to me when you've cleaned them all." We had learned our first lesson: when sergeants are wandering around collecting men, pick up anything in sight and look busy.

The city was teeming with a marvelous, heterogeneous collection: wounded from the British Army, stragglers from the Belgian Army, refugees, French reservists, British Army Service Corps units—all wandering around the streets aimlessly, some terribly depressed, others hilarious and singing, and a good portion of them drunk.

*Legion material,—August, 1914.*

*A month later.*

## WAR FEVER

We sat down in a café by the river, but before our drinks came some one had started a row. There were no windows or doors in front, just one huge corrugated iron shutter, so when the trouble began the proprietor simply pulled down the shutter. Naturally, feeling that they were shut off from the police, the trouble-makers redoubled their efforts. Then the *patron* made his second blunder: he put out the lights. Something whizzed past my ear and exploded with the noise of a shell. A woman screamed like a horse, evidently cut by glass from the siphon which someone had hurled, and hell broke out in the dark.

Five minutes later the police were hammering on the iron front and prying it open with crowbars. There was a moment's silence until they had lifted it high enough for a man to pass under, and then came the inevitable rush for freedom. Glasses, tables, chairs and police went down under the onslaught, and in thirty seconds the café had emptied itself into the street.

At reveille next morning, we were told to prepare to leave in an hour's time, and two hours later we were awaiting entrainment at the station.

## TEN THOUSAND SHALL FALL

By this time there were four companies of new recruits. Drawn up on the station platform, they presented a mixed spectacle as far as equipment went. The first company had drawn *bougerons,* (coarse linen blouses and trousers used for work in the French Army) and *képis* (caps). The second had *képis,* but the only thing uniform about the third and fourth companies was the regulation French Army blanket, carried in a roll over one shoulder, and the Army *quart* (tin cup) tied with string to the end of the blanket roll.

Fifty-six into forty—even without the eight horses—makes the only possible position, a half squatting one, until some climb out on the roof. Four days of this in the middle of August.

At the beginning of the trip, large tins of Bully Beef were issued, containing enough meat for one man for four days. The weather was hot, so we were told to form groups of four and open one tin a day amongst us. The Russian volunteers, however, were somewhat suspicious of one another, and each one cherished and opened his own tin the first day. All went well till the beginning of the third day when most of them came down with ptomaine; and by the

## WAR FEVER

morning of the fourth, they were being taken out of the wagons dead. This, and the constant fights to fill our water bottles at the various stations, served to keep up interest in military life.

We arrived after sundown on the fourth day. The companies fell in on the station platform and moved off smartly, in columns of four through the streets of Toulouse toward the barracks of the 183rd Infantry. We felt a certain amount of pride as we marched out, for each nationality of volunteers had its own country's flag in the group. Surely the good citizens of Toulouse would appreciate our *beau geste,* and realize we were there of our own volition! To our amazement and chagrin, the column was greeted with hoots and boos, and presently apples, rotten eggs, and even dead cats. I was totally bewildered till I began to pick out some of the invectives hurled at us.

"*Ah, les brigands! Salles Boches! En v'la des prisonniers!*" Brigands, Huns. Some prisoners!

I realized then they mistook us for German prisoners. It was impossible for the officers and non-coms to make that howling mob understand the real situation, so we ploughed through our baptism of fire to the security of the barracks square. Here we were allotted to rooms, and, luxury of luxuries, beds again.

In spite of four days in a truck, I tossed and pitched all night and woke in the morning convinced of a high fever. One look at the bites and marks on my chest, however, calmed this suspicion, but aroused another. I picked up the end of the barrack cot, and letting it down again with a bump, could actually hear them as they plopped on the floor and scuttled for cover. The old timers knew what to do. After coffee a crusade started, and every bed was scorched by improvised torches and then painted with kerosene. The straw in the *sacs à viande* (coarse canvas bags filled with straw used as mattresses) was burned, and the bags themselves boiled.

There were thirty-two men in the room. In the bed on my right was an American of French origin, one Phelizot, who had spent most of his life as a professional elephant hunter, round Lake Tchad. To my left a Belgian butcher with a mania for ripening little cheeses under his mattress. This, and a fixed idea on his part that it was dangerous to open the windows at

## WAR FEVER

night, leagued Phelizot and me together in a struggle for fresh air. Three times during the night I woke half suffocated and opened the window. Finally we rose together, and advancing on the sleeping Belgian, each hurled one of his boots through the panes of the fast-closed window. Then we slept, in spite of the coughs sneezes and curses of our cheese-cuddling neighbor.

Barrack life began; but no one knew to what regiment the volunteers had been assigned. The training was carried on by old reserve officers, and one or two corporals and sergeants from the Foreign Legion.

Drawing uniforms and equipment was comic. We were marched off by sections (sixty men) to the magazine. Here harried *sous-officiers* passed us out weird garments: uniforms, belts, buckles, shoes and caps, and we felt like Christmas trees as we staggered out.

Back in the barrack room things began to take some sort of order. The *capote* (great coat) had to be folded and placed first on the shelf above the beds, then the *vareuses* (shell jackets) and so on, until the pile was some three feet high. The belts, cartridge pouches and bayonets hung on hooks below, and any private belongings had to be hidden in the bed or behind the pile of uniforms.

That day a detail was marched into the arsenal to bring back rifles, which were stacked in the arm racks at the end of the room. Route march training began. Every day the distance was increased and the loads were heavier. By the end of a fortnight the recruits were able to do at least twenty miles a day with full African Army equipment of a hundred pounds.

Headed by a drum-and-bugle band, a battalion of bearded *Légionaires* marched into the barracks square, stacked arms, and were divided amongst the three battalions of volunteers. By nightfall they had sold the eager recruits all their spare equipment, and two days later they had it all back again.

There are certain hard and fast rules in the Legion. To take money or valuables is stealing. To sneak equipment or any Government issue from your own section or squad is neither etiquette nor healthy. Otherwise, you can shift for yourself.*

Having bought the same blouses twice from

*This is called System D. *(Debrouillez-vous)*

## WAR FEVER

two different *Légionaires,* Phelizot and I planned a come back. Regulations required a *Légionaire* to wear all his decorations on full dress parade and this rule was carefully checked. Our method was simple. These medals were for sale not to be worn, but as souvenirs; also they were easy to hang on to, so that by buying and holding them one could sell at exorbitant rates before dress parade, thereby breaking even.

The French Army is sufficiently fed but only just. The *bleus* (recruits) are always hungry; you even see recruits scraping the squad soup kettles to get a little extra. As time goes on, their appetites fall off and the old timers eat about half the rations served out to them, saving the rest for future reference.

The first meal—four in the morning—is a cup of black coffee, sweetened, if the cook and the quarter-master corporal have not been able to swap sugar for wine, otherwise not. No bread is issued in the morning. At eleven, comes the heavy meal of the day: soup with bread and meat in it, one cup of coffee and one cup of wine; at five, more meat made into a goulash with potatoes, beans, lentils or rice, and another cup of coffee and wine. This fare is occasionally varied, especially in the field where sections can draw and cook their own rations. The bread—one loaf per day—is coarse peasant bread, and heavily seasoned with saltpeter, for obvious reasons, stamped with the date of baking. Theoretically, you can refuse it after the tenth day, but refusal merely means self-denial.

In time of peace, you have tin plates, knives, forks and spoons, but war-time equipment is simpler: a *gamelle* (tin-plated bowl with a tight cover, that is strapped at the top of the pack), a tin cup, called a *quart,* alleged to hold a quarter of a litre, and a fork and spoon.

The food is all heaped into your *gamelle,* and coffee poured into your cup when you have finished your wine. *Pinard* (red army wine) is brought in, in a canvas bucket and ladled out with the corporal's cup, into each individual cup. By placing his thumb well down into his cup, in giving out wine to the half section, (thirty men) he can come out ahead, to the amount displaced by thirty thumbs. There is always a yell, and always the same excuse given: the canvas bucket leaks—although the buckets are usually so thickly covered with grease and grime that they

## WAR FEVER

could hold live steam under thirty pounds pressure. The only way to prevent this cheating is to watch the deal. At the front, during the winter months, a quarter of a cup of rum is issued at daybreak, but no one dare take liberties with this.

The emergency rations were as follows: two cans of preserved meat known as *singe* (monkey), twenty biscuits and a small bag of sugar and coffee. The latter was carefully checked at all inspections—"unauthorized use of reserve rations: eight days prison." This did not deter us from making coffee on the sly, as inspections took place in double rank and it was easy to cheat. All full sacks of coffee and sugar were lent to men in the front rank, and as the officer inspected and passed on, they were flipped back to the rear rank, to be inspected a second time as their turn came. Biscuits were as hard as rock, unless you knew the trick. No amount of soaking affected them, but put them in the oven or near the fire, and you could almost eat them. As for tobacco—considered as firewood it wasn't bad. Every ten days the Government issued a package per man, called *Scafarlati des Troupes*. It was mostly the stalks of tobacco plants, and you had to spread it on a handkerchief, pick out the longer pieces, and chop them up before you could possibly roll it into a cigarette. Hardly worth the trouble as it was poisonous stuff, anyway.

The barrack rooms became orderly, even quiet at night: the Legion cure for snoring is crude but effective. When they are sure the offender is asleep, two men picked for the job gently varnish his lips and close them. On waking, his mouth is firmly sealed, and the first unwary yawn tears strips of skin and flesh from both lips. Once or twice is enough. The victim takes his own precautions not to snore, even if he has to bind up his jaw with a handkerchief.

As recruits we drew the magnificent sum of one *sou* a day. It did not spell luxury, so it was possible, if you had the cash, to hire old *Légionaires* to do anything from cleaning your rifle to replacing you on guard duty if you wanted to go in town. But this scale of pay did not apply to men in their second and third enlistments. There were privates of fifteen and seventeen years' standing, who, thanks to the bonus for reenlistment and high pay for previous service, were drawing two and three francs a day.

## WAR FEVER

Non-commissioned officers were forbidden to borrow money from their subordinates, but most of them did, especially the corporals. It was not bad policy to lend, even if you never expected to see the money back. They rarely borrowed twice from the same man, and it certainly greased the wheels. Strictly speaking sergeants could not drink with soldiers. Occasionally they would graciously drink off a proffered glass in passing a table, but to sit down at that table was beneath their dignity. Regulations are all very well, but what's the use of stripes if you can't profit by 'em?

Dry-nursed by the old *Légionaires* we began to shape up. Within three weeks, stiffened by three hundred *anciens* per battalion and the *cadre* of regular officers and non-coms, we were ready for service.

We were a job lot, for the most part Russian, Swiss, Belgian and English, though almost every neutral nation was represented. Some were there for the adventure, others from a sense of obligation to France, or because they could not get back to their own countries to join up, and quite a number because the war had thrown them out of a job. The old *Légionaires* were made of quite different stuff and were in it for reasons ranging from man-slaughter to unrequited love. It struck me as strange, at first, that there were even Germans and Turks among the *anciens*.

Vetman, the corporal of our squad, had been a Prussian guardsman in his day, but some dispute with a superior had forced him to desert and take refuge in the Legion. Where else could he go? Born and bred to soldiering, it was the only life he knew or cared about, *"Che foutrais être un bombier à Baris"**—This was his highest ambition. Tall, scraggy, and ungainly, except on parade ground, he was the typical soldier, and his lank form was tireless. Though a strict disciplinarian he had unlimited patience with stupid recruits. It was true he had been in the German Army, but after seventeen years' service in Africa the French considered him a *Légionaire,* and their confidence was justified. He was killed six months later defending an exposed outpost.

Thérisien, a Breton, was my ideal of a *sous-*

*His way of pronouncing "I would like to be a Paris fireman."

*officier*. He had been a lieutenant in the Navy. A fit of temper, a hasty blow, and cashiered! He buried himself in the Legion. With his ability and previous rank he soon rose to the grade of *aspirant* (cadet officer). Another hasty blow, and back to the ranks again. Now he was sergeant once more. He could do what he liked with us, and his lectures on field tactics were worthy of a colonel. These were the best types but not the most amusing.

Conti, an Italian, offered to show me the ropes and valet me. He was a likable sort of rogue, but things had an unfortunate habit of disappearing. When my tooth brush went I put him through a third degree.

"Conti, what did you do in civilian life?"

"Me? I pinched bikes."

"Do you mean to say you were a bicycle thief?"

"Sure, that was my profession and my father's before me." Such talent was beyond my means.

Most of us Americans were in the same section, 57 varieties. My closest friends Phil, the elephant hunter, Denny Dowd, a lawyer from New York, Fritz—, an engineer, Stuart—, an

## TEN THOUSAND SHALL FALL

artist, and Alan*—, our dreamy, but martial, poet.

Going into town was not so simple as it sounds. Every man had to pass the inspection of the sergeant-of-the-guard at the gate. Brass buttons must shine, boots, if not polished, be neatly greased; the broad blue woolen belt of the Legion must be wound around without a crease, and, as it was nine feet long, this was quite an accomplishment. If the sergeant happened to be in bad humor a man might be told to go back two or three times to make good minute defects. Coming back was easier, as all returned together. But even so, the lynx-eyed sergeant was on the watch for any men he considered sufficiently drunk to shove into the *boîte* (prison).

Re this, it was an amazing sight to see some of the old timers. They would reel up the street roaring obscene songs, at the tops of their lungs. Twenty yards before they came to the gate the songs ceased, shoulders went back, and they would march through the gate, saluting smartly like automatons. Out of sight of the guard the

---

*Editor's Note: The reference here and later is to Alan Seeger, the poet who wrote the "Rendez-vous With Death," shortly before being killed in action.

## WAR FEVER

singing would break out anew, as they zig-zagged across the yard and lurched up the stairway to their barrack room.

I wangled my way into a *peleton de sous-off* (school for non-coms), and soon regretted it. There were no privileges, and lots of extra work, and chances of promotion in the immediate future were slim.

*Chapter Two*

## MOVING UP AND SHAKING DOWN

ALARUMS *and excursions!* The Powers-that-Be had decided to send off one battalion at once. Five hundred old *Légionaires* and five hundred volunteers picked from those with previous military experience. I wracked my brain and finally remembered the Columbia Institute Military Academy in New York. I was only seven at that time, but the words *école militaire* work wonders in France; and that night I was in the *premier bataillon de marche,* likely to be sent to the front any day.

Nothing happened for three days, but we put on an extra amount of swank which we mistook for *esprit de corps*. Late one afternoon, town leave was refused, and we were assembled in the barracks square for kit inspection. Next morning, headed by the drum-and-bugle band, flowers in the muzzles of our rifles, we were cheered through the town to the station.

## MOVING UP

"*40-8's*" once more, but this time what a difference! Forty men, and forty men only, to a truck. Two climbed in, and the rifles and sacks of the other thirty-eight were passed up to them, and stacked at both ends of the car. The rest of us piled in; corporals stood in the doors to prevent anyone leaving, and the train pulled out. At the first big station the cars spewed forth food-seeking *Légionaires* like a disturbed ant hill; and we got our first inkling of what the rest of the world thought of the Legion.

We headed for the buffet to buy provisions, but the door was slammed in our faces by an enormously fat *chef de gare,* who then rushed down the platform shouting at the top of his lungs, "*Fermez toutes les portes! Voici la Légion!*" Scouting around, we found a canteen in a tent behind the station, and after a struggle we bought sausages and white bread and returned to our car, hurt and indignant at the attitude of the authorities.

The train pulled out of the station, and the *anciens* pulled out their loot. From under blankets, like rabbits from a hat, came a prodigious supply of food and drink—

# TEN THOUSAND SHALL FALL

"  . . . . . . . . .
More beer, in little kegs,
Many dozen hard boiled eggs,
And goodies to a fabulous amount."

No deception—quite simple. Merely a matter of slitting the back of the tent, and helping themselves, while we—innocent decoys—engaged the enemy over the counter. Maybe that *chef de gare* wasn't so far wrong after all! We thought this was worthy of commemoration in song, so, to the tune of the Boys in Blue are Marching:

We are the famous Legion
That they talk so much about.
People lock up everything
Whenever we're about.

We're noted for our pillaging,
The nifty way we steal.
We'd pinch a baby carriage,
And the infant, for a meal!

As we go marching,
And the band begins to play—Gor'blimee!
You can hear the people shouting,
Lock all the doors, shut up the shop,
            the Legion's here to-day.

## MOVING UP

At the Camp de Mailly we saw the effects of shell fire for the first time. The iron shutters of the station were riddled with shrapnel and some of the buildings demolished. Decidedly, we were getting nearer the war. The next day we were sent out to round up some Uhlans hiding in the woods. They had been cut off during the retreat, and had managed to exist on their iron rations, raw vegetables and anything else they could steal, hoping to lie hidden till the German Army should advance once more, and free them. They were a sullen crowd, gaunt and ragged, but we admired their pluck.

It was at the Camp de Mailly, that *Monsieur Toto et Cie.* made his first public appearance. He probably came from the Arabs in the Legion —the Koran extends a closed game season to cooties. It was the irony of fate that our poet should be the first to complain of the roughness of army underwear. For several days Alan scratched body and soul in forced aloofness, but there was no avoiding them. From that time, like the poor, they were always with us. How Alan must have suffered! He took them as seriously as he did everything else. I never saw him laugh. He was always scribbling and occasionally showed me the results. At the time I didn't realize he meant his "Rendez-vous With Death," in earnest. He could fight as well as write though, but that comes later. . . .

Then the march to the front began; thirty-five kilometres a day, with full equipment. The first night our squad was in luck; no sore feet, and billeted in a real house. The old lady who owned it was horrified at the idea of our sleeping on bare boards, and produced four enormous eiderdowns.

The next day brought out the real discipline of the Legion. There is no issue of socks in the French Army, and the *bleus* began to suffer. You can either put your boots on bare-footed, or use little squares of cheap muslin, *(chausettes russes)*. Placing your foot in the middle of it, you wrap the muslin carefully around the foot and ankle and slide into the shoe. This sounds simple, but it takes months of practice to do, without having the cloth shift and the feet blister. Those of us who could afford socks had chosen them badly and Stuart and I were suffering acutely. Our shoes felt as if they were filled with painful marmalade, and we fell out by the side of the road to investigate. Sure

## MOVING UP

enough—they were blistered and bleeding. We decided we were fit cases for the ambulance. This illusion, however, was rudely shattered by a bull voice coming from the top of a horse.

*"Que faites vous là?"*

Heroically, we stood up, saluted our colonel and exhibited the pitiful spectacle of our feet.

*"Nos pattes sont en marmalade, mon colonel. Nous ne pouvons plus marcher."* ("Our dogs are cut to ribbons, colonel. We're all in.")

Revolver, in hand, he roared, *"Marchez quand même!"* And we did, rejoining our section at the double.

The night was spent in the arcades of a monastery; where Vetman took us in hand and showed us what to do for our feet.*

Stuart and I had it out, in the morning.

"Look here, Cocky—I'll carry a razor if you'll pack the blades."

"All right—and one mirror will do for both

---

*The Legion cures blisters by passing a greased thread through them, cutting the ends off each side—this acts as a drain. They then smear the whole inflamed part with tallow, also the outside of the sock, to prevent chafing. This done, they put their boots on again—painful, but easier than doing it next morning when feet have had a chance to swell.

of us. What's more, I don't see the use of keeping a hair brush."

"What about this packet of Bromo paper—can't we split it?"

"Oh, all right—be fussy! But the sooner you ask your friends to write you on thin, soft paper the better!"

"How in Hell can I?"

"Kid 'em along: tell 'em you like to carry their letters with you, to read over—"

A two day march had taught us that possessions are a curse—Other bright volunteers had reached the same conclusion, and the shower of safety razors, mirrors, combs, extra soap, shirts, and underclothes was eagerly seized upon by the old timers.

The third day we hit the little town of Verzy near Epernay. This was on the front. The town itself was on raised ground, and the edge of it, looking over the green vineyards, was like a quay by the sea. About three miles from the town were front line trenches, and we all crowded into the streets to see the shells bursting till an enemy plane went over, and we were driven back into quarters, like chickens when a hawk hovers near. Rumors began to fly

## MOVING UP

again: we were going into line that night—we were to attack—etc. ad nauseam.

In the meantime we were confined to billets during the day. Our company was quartered in some long sheds used by the grape gatherers during the vintage, and we slept on concrete platforms, which sloped toward the middle of the room, divided by low partitions like stalls in a modern stable. The *anciens* found wine, and the night was made hideous by song, drunken laughter, and squabbles. African troops had been there before us, and we were given a warm welcome by the Algerian Cooties' Rotary Club.

Here we waited for orders to join some Army Corps, but the various generals seemed to think the Legion might corrupt the morals or discipline of their troops. Anyway, there was no ugly rush to take us over.

One morning motor trucks appeared out of nowhere, and all that day Battalion C rolled along the roads to Fismes. We arrived just at nightfall and our section being the section of the day, went on ahead to act as *campement* (billeting party) for the rest.

The battalion was to be quartered at a little

village called Cuiry les Chaudards, but in the dark we must have passed beside it, and struck the first line. In those days there were no trenches or barbed wire. The first intimation we had of our mistake was a salvo of 77's from the enemy's batteries. The shells were high and burst some hundred yards behind us. The old *Légionaires,* and the men who had seen service before, flopped on their stomachs. The rest of us stood dumb-founded, for a moment, and then, in our ignorance, began to laugh at the nervousness of the veterans. The main thing proved, however, was that the section was off its course, so we retraced our steps and eventually found the village, with the battalion already installed and the major furious.

The night was restless. Violent fusillades broke out in the line in front of us, and each time, our *sous-officiers,* accustomed to the suddenness of Moroccan warfare, had us stand to arms.

Our squad was quartered in the attic of a one-story house, and hostile relations with the owners were established immediately. In the first place, they bitterly resented our efforts to clean up the quagmire and dunghill in the farmyard. Nor were matters smoothed over by the fact that a

## MOVING UP

bed-ridden grandmother had been drenched during the night by a *Légionaire* too drunk or too lazy to find his way down the ladder into the farmyard. Also, we found out later, this family and three others were in communication with the enemy, and naturally, thirty men snooping around cramped their style.

Cuiry les Chaudards was a small farming village, which in summer was entirely surrounded by fields of crops, and in winter by mud. It boasted some forty surly inhabitants, of whom, one or two of the more enterprising had opened little shops in their houses. They were driving an amazing trade in sweet biscuits, infamous tin-canned jam, and *vin mousseux*. The *caporal ordinaire* (quarter-master corporal) took a wagon to Fismes every day, and could be bribed to buy extras there. Such were the luxuries of life. The labors consisted of drills, manoeuvres, digging a second line of trenches, carrying logs for struts and shores, and cleaning up the village.

I was flat—*fauché*—broke! At Cuiry les Chaudards they mistook my American gold pieces for gold bricks. It hurt to plunk my last few francs into soap, but the laundry business

## TEN THOUSAND SHALL FALL

seemed the only industrial opening for a bright young man, so I went into partnership with a Norwegian architect. Down by the river, the day's work was divided:

"All right, Henri, my turn to wash—Where's the soap?"

"I put it in your haversack." Scrub—scrub—

"Here—rinse these, and spread 'em on that log—No—not the rock. Picot's got his stuff too near it—he'd pinch ours."

"Dave, where is the *Adjudant's* shirt?"

"I gave it to you to dry. For God's sake—didn't you watch it? There goes Conti! Catch him, and tell him you want it back."

Five minutes later Henri returned with the shirt—Conti had made a slight mistake in picking up his wash! And so it went on—business throve—if you watched while you washed.

\* \* \* \* \* \*

"*Faites les sacs—Tout le monde en bas! Les sous-offs au capitaine—et grouillez—vous!*"\*
A brief consultation with the major, the captains joined their companies, and we moved off through the night, in column of twos. We soon

---

\*"Make your packs,—everybody turn out! Sergeants call. Make it snappy!"

*My partner in the laundry business.*

## MOVING UP

left the metaled roads for a lane through the woods, and there struck one of the real horrors of war—mud. Liquid mud—full of treacherous roots. Mud like chewing gum—squelching—sucking our boots off. Mud with a stench obscene and putrid—Black mud—black night. Somebody down. Up again, cursing foully . . . We were in Indian file now, picking our way by the sky-line of the trees . . . . Hours and hours we floundered through the pit black night. Then suddenly we were through the woods.

Shadows rose out of the ground—whispered hurried directions and warnings, disappeared into the night. We slipped into the rifle pits.

With the dawn came reaction. The peaceful landscape hardly seemed to justify last night's caution, and five *bleus* wandered off in the sunshine to see where the war was.

They saw nothing . . . .

Three of them probably never even heard the shell. You see, we wore red trousers in those days—they were beautiful targets. We paid high for the thoughtlessness of the five as the sector came in for an hour's heavy shelling.

There was no barbed wire as yet, so at nightfall covering patrols were sent out into No Man's

## TEN THOUSAND SHALL FALL

Land, I went out with one commanded by an American soldier of fortune, veteran of Spanish-American-Philippine, and Mexican campaigns—he was a good soldier, but slightly erratic and impatient. The long, cold vigil on the ground exasperated him—we were all pretty jumpy. About midnight the moon began to show through the clouds and my heart skipped a beat. "Christ—here they come!" Stealing silently up the slope in skirmish order were ten or twelve shadowy forms. A warning hiss from Sergeant Morlae, and we retired to our lines to report.

"Every one up—Load—Commence firing!"

Denny and I held our fire, waiting to see something to shoot at, congratulating ourselves on our coolness. This, however, called down the wrath of the top sergeant, who told us in no gentle manner to fire level with the ground till we could pick our shots. The enemy replied. A gale of bullets whistled overhead, and we could see the flashes of rifles towards the left of the line. This went on for half an hour; then firing stopped, and an old Legion sergeant volunteered to go out and reconnoiter.

Half an hour later he came back convulsed with mirth. The enemy we had seen proved to

## MOVING UP

be twelve cows grazing between the lines, of which nine had paid the full penalty. The firing came from another battalion of the Legion that had come up and occupied the edge of the woods in front of us, forming one side of a V with our own lines. Naturally, these trenches were dubbed les *Tranchées des Vaches*.

The officers believed in having the field kitchens as near the front line as possible; consequently, a magnificent emplacement was dug for the *hash guns*. A German plane circled overhead, and half an hour later Fritz, having mistaken the kitchen for a battery, proceeded to demolish it, just as grub was ready. More casualties and no soup. The kitchens were moved back and soup details became a nightmare. Stumbling through the woods, sliding and falling in the mud, with two kettles full of hot, greasy stew or a bucket of coffee to fill one's cup of bliss. How we loved our enemies!

*Ajudant Pellotti was a Corsican; there were a lot of them in the Legion. He was a thick set,

*The grade of *Ajudant* is the equivalent of Battalion Sergeant Major in our army. What we call an Adjutant the French call *Capitaine adjoint*. (Captain attached to the Colonel) usually the senior Captain, in line for his majority.

coarse little swine with homo-sexual tendencies, and had been bothering the life out of a big, mild sort of fellow called Marco. When Marco ignored the sly pats and pinches Pellotti made his life Hell, in a hundred and one ways, as a sous-officier can and still keep within regulations. The night of the relief we were in high spirits, in spite of the march before us. Marco had a good, trained voice, and was giving vent to his feelings in song. Suddenly the men behind him were pushed aside as Pellotti bustled forward. Whipping out his revolver, he shoved it into Marco's ribs.

"*Sacre cabotin de bordel*—singing again! Stop that bloody row or I'll blow your liver through your backbone! Shut up!"

Marco shut up: the threats and abuse went on. Nothing was said, but somewhere behind Pellotti there were three ominous clicks, the noise of breech bolts being snapped closed as three cartridges went home. Pellotti fairly hurled himself to the front of the line. It was too easy for somebody to stumble and have a rifle go off by accident in that dark, muddy labyrinth. The hint was enough.

Men will forgive much in a brave and efficient

## MOVING UP

*sous-officicr.* Pellotti was neither. Once during rifle inspection a victim of his persecutions, maddened by *cafard*,* threw up his rifle and fired at him point-blank. Unfortunately, he missed the ajudant and killed a corporal standing nearby. A night came, however, when Pellotti took out a reconnoitering patrol. He advanced a certain distance into No Man's Land, and ordered them to proceed while he waited for them. Half an hour later he crawled back, dying, with three French bullets in him. The rest of his patrol had lost their bearings and mistaken him for a German outpost. At least, that was their story, and they stuck to it.

*Cafard* comes from the word meaning "black beetle." In Army jargons it means blues or melancholia. The African Army troops are very subject to this periodically, due probably to the heat and bad wine. In the more acute cases the victims are convinced that their brains are being eaten by black beetles.

*Chapter Three*
# IN FOR KEEPS

In the early part of the war troops were scarce, and reliefs were few, and far between. I have done as much as twenty-eight days at a stretch in the first line. Often our rest was merely a few days in the second line dugouts. The word "rest" was euphemistic. By the end of ten days digging trenches, building dugouts, cutting and carrying enormous logs of wood and barbed wire, we were quite ready to go up into line again.

During one of these rest cures, Denny and I came down with dysentery, and were too weak to crawl when the battalion moved up. Nobody seemed to care. The Sergeant mumbled something about reporting to the doctor, and we were left alone in a little hut in the woods. Two days later we managed to drag ourselves to our infirmary to beg some opium pills, but found, to our horror, the medical staff of another battalion. There was no way to get medicine or food, nor

## IN FOR KEEPS

was there anyone to vouch for us. We suddenly realized that if anyone in authority should question us they would consider us deserters—so we beat a hasty retreat. We lived like hunted animals; stealing what we could from the kitchens after dark, and hiding whenever we saw an officer or a sergeant. The third day a cyclist from our own battalion turned up, and we went up into line with him that night.

It was only November, 1914, but we realized that trench warfare had come to stay. In two months the rifle pits of the Marne had spread into a complicated system of trenches, dugouts, machine gun emplacements. Finally, a vast web of barbed wire was spun along the whole front.

Our new sector was called Oulch on the map, Picadilly Circus by the English volunteers, and the *fer à cheval* (horseshoe) by the Legion. We found ourselves in a sort of quarry with well-made dugouts built into the chalk above it. There was no further need of covering patrols at night, thanks to the barbed wire, but the sector was much more heavily bombarded than the last, so we remained under cover when not on duty.

The machine gun section was, naturally, installed in the strongest dugout—machine guns cost money.  We saw what an **H-E 105″** could do when a lucky shot passed through the loophole and burst clean inside.  Our squad rushed in to help the survivors—there were none—so we set to work to clear up the mess.  I was struck by the practical coolness of an old *Légionaire* who was transferring a mess of blood and brains from the floor into a *képi* with the late owner's spoon.

In our off moments we told the stories of our lives—usually mythical—and read our shirts.

We had a crude chimney in our dugout and were busy brewing chocolate.  Bert, from Kentucky, ex-racing driver, and God knows what besides, was going all out.  He finished, and there was a moment of awed silence.  His sidekick broke the spell:

"Bert," (scratch) "you know that's a damned lie."  (scratch) (scratch).

The answer was disarming.  "Well, who the hell said it wasn't!"

Here Bill's wriggling and scratching disturbed the aesthetic artist beside him.  Turning his face from the fire, with a dreamy look in his eye, he summed up the whole cootie question:

"Good Lord, Bill!  Do you still *scratch*!"

## IN FOR KEEPS

The nights were more fun. The Boches used to sneak out and hang baskets of "delicatessen" on our wire. There was always a note with them, assuring us this was their daily fare, and we need only desert to enjoy the same. Our officers replied in kind. But we felt that Charity began at home, and the baskets were generally empty by the time they reached the German wire.

\* \* \* \* \* \*

It gave us comfort and cheer to see the Château lighted as we filed through the gates of the park. The glass porte-cochère was intact, and so little damage seemed to have been done to the facade that it was hard to realize we were only a few hundred yards from the front line. We turned the corner, and as if by black magic the lights went out, and the place became a gutted ruin. It had only been the moon shining through empty windows. The heavily vaulted cellars had resisted shrapnel and fire; and here our company was quartered. One section was immediately posted at points of vantage along the wall of the park where rude shelters had been built; and the wall itself was loopholed.

Craonnelle must have been taken by surprise

in the opening days of the war. I don't know how the inhabitants fared, but a baleful feeling lurked about the ruins. I couldn't wait to explore. The gatekeeper's lodge had not been shelled but the interior was indescribably filthy. The Hun had evidently had one last banquet here. A long table in the main room was piled high with dirty dishes, wine glasses and bottles, and he had left his usual trade mark—excrement —on everything. In the middle of this débris of debauch, lay a small white satin slipper. Evidently Fritz had been true to his traditions of the Kürfürstendam. Had the owner escaped? My mind went back to my mother's place, in France—not so far from the tide of invasion— and I was damned glad I was in the show.

The position at Craonnelle was somewhat precarious. All the streets were heavily barricaded, as half the town was held by the enemy. During the first month of the Legion's occupation it changed hands repeatedly, but we gradually cleared it and consolidated the position.

A barricade at the end of a street is a tricky thing to hold. The attackers have most of the advantage. They mass their forces around the corner and charge in a concerted rush, giving

## IN FOR KEEPS

the defenders time for but one shot apiece. Grenades were still unknown, and machine guns too precious to waste on outpost duty. Our major *(commandant)* solved the problem, however, by raking the country-side for shot guns; and these, loaded with slugs, shot and old nails, proved most effective against sudden rushes.

Then the Germans—it was a regiment of *Jägers*—pulled their first raid. Half our section had gone down to draw rations for the week, leaving the other two squads to guard the wall of the park. Vetman, and the man off duty, were in a little shelter in a corner of the wall. Kiffen Rockwell and Alan were doing sentry-go along the wall itself—that is to say, on planks supported by barrels. Suddenly Kiff saw a spark come over the wall from outside.

"You see that, Alan?"

"Yes, I saw that. Do you think it was a bomb?"

"Yes, I think it was a bomb. We'd better call Vetman—" (B-o-o-o-o-o-m !!!) "My God, it *was* a bomb!"

Clearly outlined above the top of the wall, they drew a fusillade from the raiders outside, which drove them off their platform. Before they had time to do anything the garden door, on their left, was blown in.

Then there was quick action. The corporal, turning out with the rest of the guard, was met by a howling rush of Germans pouring through the shattered gate. A short hand-to-hand; and Vetman, seeing he was outnumbered, ordered his men to the cover of the park skirting the inside of the wall. As he gave the command his brains were dashed out by the butt of a Boche rifle. The Germans had just time to strip the dead of all their papers, regimental badges, etc., before the section returned from the food detail and drove them out.

Sentinels were doubled and everybody in the section was on guard duty along the wall. About an hour later, we heard something new, but very old. Down from the German lines, on the crest across the valley, came a long wolf-like howl, half human, half beast—derision, triumph, and revenge—straight back across the ages from ape-man and wolf-pack. They had found out that Vetman was a deserter, and war and exultation had stripped the Hun of all veneer and boasted *Kultur*.

Phélizot said it first.

## IN FOR KEEPS

"Well, fellows, we're in it for keeps. Let's start a little raid of our own."

Towards morning I disgraced myself. As dawn broke, I was looking through a loophole with the wind blowing in my face, and I made the fatal mistake of resting my chin on my arms. A sniper's bullets smacked the wall just over the loophole, and off I toppled, rolling on the ground. The concern of the sergeant who ran to pick me up changed to wrath when he realized that I had been dozing. Fortunately, the regulations of the French Army insist that you cannot be shot for sleeping at your post after four hours' continual guard, but there is no regulation to prevent every filthy detail of a company being heaped upon you for weeks afterward.

Two nights later we moved up to the "sky parlor," as we dubbed the sector on the hill overlooking the *château*. Here Phélizot organized his raid but did not see fit to inform the *sous-officiers* of his intentions.

I have said before that Phélizot was an elephant hunter, and a successful one, for he had made a fair-sized fortune in ivory. As he explained it the difficulty and danger was not in shooting elephants, but in dodging the Belgian,

## TEN THOUSAND SHALL FALL

French and British game wardens over their respective borders in the process of poaching, which crime he freely admitted. His only fear seemed to be of himself, yet he was extraordinarily tolerant of weakness and failings in others.

The first time Phil went out, he tried to bring back a German sentry, smothering his yells in a blanket. There were too many others nearby, however, and he almost got shot up for his pains. He would use all his skill as a hunter to bring himself within striking range of the quarry, but once there, would risk his own life, rather than chance killing a man with a crack on the head. I told him he was crazy to try such stunts, but he only smiled—

"You see, Dave, in the game I was in, you're killing, or spilling blood every day. If it isn't an elephant, it's game for the boys, or just slaughtering a goat for meat. It seems to get into you, after a while, the everlasting shooting and blood; and men get what they call Blood Fever. Some of my friends got it—The natives get on your nerves and you start knocking them around with a jambok and draw blood. Then one day you lose your temper and shoot one. I felt it coming on, so I quit and came home." The

## IN FOR KEEPS

horror of it was so strong that he could not bring himself to kill a man single handed, even in war.

The next night he took me with him. It was eerie work, crawling toward the German lines, especially when we came to the zone where the corpses of the first big battles lay, still unburied. On we went, freezing when a star shell went up, crawling forward again immediately afterward, in the accentuated darkness. I was no big game hunter, but, by putting my hands and feet exactly in the tracks of Phélizot, managed to slide along quite quietly. Would we ever reach the German lines—? The answer was a sharp clank twenty yards behind me. Looking back, my heart almost stopped. There, large as life, and twice as ugly, was a German sentinel, standing with his back to me. I shook Phil's foot and pointed. But the only reaction was a whispered explanation: "Yes, I know. That's the second one."

My teeth chattered with reassurance.

Finally we came to a communication trench and here Phil got much excited. He pointed out a fresh spoor of German feet in the mud and proposed to wait, one on each side of the trench, till he, or they, returned. Then I was to crack the last man over the head as he went by, and we would take him back to our lines.

Unfortunately this plan was upset by the lateness of the hour, so we started back. Nothing happened till we got within thirty yards of our outpost, when considering all danger past we rose to our feet and started walking in, talking as we went. Ordinarily it is easy enough to distinguish between English and German; but after two hours of guard duty, an excitable Italian is apt to confuse the two, especially coming from the direction of the enemy's lines. We were greeted by a hasty *"Halte là! Qui vive?"* giving us just time to flop, before it was followed up by a bullet. Recognition finally established we got back to the lines. Here the plot thickened.

Jaeger, the man promoted to replace Vetman, was a red-headed hot-tempered Alsacian who took his new stripes seriously.

"Where have you two been?"

"Oh, just over the German lines to have a look around."

"Oh, you have, have you! You think you can go out and come back when you like in this Army? Did anyone give you orders to go on

## IN FOR KEEPS

patrol? *Silence!* Did you ask anybody's permission even? SHUT UP! Am I commanding here, or do you think you are running it? What have you got to say for yourselves? SHUT UP! I'm talking now. I've a good mind to report you as deserters. Never heard of such crust. So you two think you are commanding this post and I count for nothing. In other words, I'm a flat-footed, lop-eared jackass, *hein?*"

Then came my chance. Drawing myself up with dignity, I quoted, "A soldier should never contradict a non-commissioned officer." He got me later on another count, but it was worth it.

\* \* \* \* \* \*

The whole front became more active. The battalions were shifted without rest from one point to another, probably to familiarize us with the various trenches. Battalion C next occupied *les Tranchées des Moulins* on the left of Berry au Bac. We were allowed to build fires in the dugouts provided we used dry wood, but one night, Flannigan, returning cold from guard duty, stoked his fire too impetuously and set the roof ablaze. When the excitement and shells had ceased I overheard two sergeants talking.

## TEN THOUSAND SHALL FALL

"*Tu sais, mon vieux, je ne suis pas sûr que ce n'était pas fait exprès. Ce Flannigan—je ne dis pas que c'est un nom boche, mais je n'en suis pas sûr.*" ("You know, old man, I am not at all sure that wasn't done on purpose. That fellow Flannigan—I don't say it's a German name, but it all looks pretty phony.")

I laughed, but not for long—fires were forbidden.

The sector had been quiet for a day or two; so a shot from an outpost roused our curiosity. Sergeant Thérisien called me and we went to investigate. We found the lone sentinel, plugged through the left arm, applying a first aid bandage. Thérisien questioned him:

"They got you, did they?"

"Yes."

"Did you see him?"

"No."

"What did you fire at?"

"I didn't fire."

"That's funny. I could have sworn it was a Lebel and not a Mauser."

The man denied it vehemently. I, too, was puzzled. I had been so sure I could tell the roar of a Lebel from the crack of a German Mauser.

## IN FOR KEEPS

Still musing, I picked up his rifle and half mechanically threw open the breech. I could have cut my hand off, but the thing was done. An empty cartridge case tinkled on the ground. Thérisien's sharp eyes spotted it. A brief search over the rampart disclosed the tell-tale bandage\*—wet, burned and blood-stained.

> "I could not look on death; this being known,
> Men led me to him blindfold, and alone."

\*A wet bandage placed outside the great coat prevents scorching, as would occur in a self-inflicted wound.

*Chapter Four*

## A CUP OF COFFEE AND A RIOT

Sergeant Major Lecomte bustled into the farmyard of our billets, and blew his whistle:

"*Rapport!* Tomorrow morning, at nine o'clock, there will be a dentist at the Regimental Infirmary. Any man who needs to see him must apply now. All those doing so will be excused from morning drill."

There was an ugly rush, and some two hundred men scrambled to put their names on the list. Something told me that this dentist was no Painless Parker, so the next morning I hung around the Infirmary door to see the fun. There they were—two hundred of them in a queue smoking and laughing, without a care in the world; all but the few who were really suffering. Suddenly the door opened, and the first man disappeared inside. There was an interested silence broken by groans and muffled curses from within. Finally the victim emerged, holding his

## COFFEE, AND A RIOT

jaw and moaning. He passed down the line spitting blood and spreading terror. The line went forward, but minus some ten or fifteen men. Again the blood-curdling sounds from within, and again the line was decimated. Coué wasn't in it! The nearer they got to the door, the surer they were their toothaches were imaginary. Six saw the dentist. The rest took two days' prison for malingering. Cheap at the price!

Next day another treat. The first company marched off to Maizy, some five miles away, for their first anti-typhoid inoculation. The march back was hellish. I wasn't the only one to crash into a dead faint as we staggered into quarters. Few of us slept that night, and the billets were like a typhoid ward in a madhouse.

Things were looking up in Cuiry les Chaudards. The social season opened with a gathering in the churchyard. For some time past, the General had noticed that this particular church had come in for a flattering amount of attention from the enemy. He organized a Field Day, to settle matters—the event of the afternoon being a tug of war. Battalion C versus Church Steeple. As the long rope tightened and the

# TEN THOUSAND SHALL FALL

steeple teetered, the inhabitants, headed by the *curé,* protested vehemently, claiming sacrilege. The General, however, was adamant. It was too good a regulating point for German guns, and he reckoned the lives of a thousand men—even godless *Légionaires*—more important than one church spire.

Two days later the battalion was marched off by companies to a nearby sugar refinery. Here shower baths had been rigged up and I had my first hot bath since Toulouse.

Just before we went up into line again three entire families were shot for conveying information to the enemy. One old man and his wife had used a pair of white oxen in their plowing to indicate the position of the French batteries, but his erratic methods of agriculture finally gave him away.

\* \* \* \* \* \*

It was Craonnelle again, this time the Little *Château* and the cemetery trenches. Interesting, but a bit grisly. The family vaults were the *parrados* of our trenches. Gradually the walls were broken down by shell fire, and now and then a wrecked coffin would slide into the trench, disgorging its occupant in various stages of de-

*Alan Seeger, Nielsen, Boligni, Morlae,--Little Chateau, Craonnelle.*

*Alan Seeger. Street of Craonnelle, November, 1914.*

## COFFEE, AND A RIOT

cay. This was stopped by boarding up the vaults, but the walls were pierced and the rats came in. It gave us the creeps to hear the greasy rustling of rats feeding inside the tombs. Later, however, chloride of lime was used; and we got no little satisfaction hearing a fat one scuttling along inside the boards, cough, choke, and retire hastily.

The Little *Château* had belonged to an old colonel. Some of it was smashed by shell fire, and ransacked for valuables; but the library had been spared. Long rows of book cases, sun pouring in on piles of magazines, and big arm chairs —a room lived in and loved. Alan and I were enthralled.

"Look here, Dave, a first edition of Jean Jacques Rousseau."

"Yes, but see this Déscartes—My God, here's Montaigne! I haven't read him since I was a kid. I used to sneak him out of the library."

"Dave, what do you make of this?"

"This" was a carefully bound manuscript, evidently the journal of the owner's grandfather, an officer on Napoleon's staff. Jena, Austerlitz, Beresina, and Moscow—what a saga! But there were other magnets—Molière, Anatole France, Farrère, Rabelais—I was miles away—

*"Rassemblement! Couvrez sur deux."* I hurtled down through the centuries to fall in for the filthiest *corvée* of my whole experience.

The captain had decided the cellar must be cleared, as a shelter in case of bombardment. During the German retreat it had evidently been used as a dressing station, bomb-proof, and finally as an arena for hand-to-hand fighting in clearing the village. The whole place was flooded two feet deep in water, for the drains had been clogged by rotting straw. As a result, the cellar, some fifteen yards square, was a huge cesspool of foul water, rotting straw and decomposed bodies. It took us a day to clean it out, but it took me a week to get the stench out of my nostrils.

Craonnelle was full of charm for the *anciens*. I found Conti, one day, coming out of the church with a secretive air, and a bulky bundle. For two weeks he lugged it around on top of his sack. Then he got confidential. After swearing me to secrecy on the heads of three generations of grandmothers, he took me into the woods and showed me the swag: three enormous gold

## COFFEE, AND A RIOT

crowns, raped from the heads of defenseless saints. Conti was gibbering with a mixture of avaricious glee and superstitious forebodings.

"*Il bello doro,*" he repeated over and over, rubbing his hands.

It was a shame to undeceive him, but I could not let him carry the crown jewels of Craonnelle any longer. I picked one up, and scraping the gilt away showed him the plaster of paris below. The chuckling ceased and superstition turned to wrath. Deep-seated, sincere rage shook him; Italian, Arabic and *Lingua-Franca* curses rolled out of his mouth, as he pulverized the crowns beneath his feet.

God had cheated him! Conti as a devout Catholic had reason to feel abused.

But to get back to Craonnelle. Bibouker, the Arab bugler, used to disappear for hours at a time. Curiosity got the better of me, and I followed him. He ducked into a house and presently a strange mechanical humming came from the top story. I crept upstairs, and for a moment had grave doubts of his sanity. There sat this great gorilla man, grinning like a death's head, and pedaling furiously on a Singer sewing machine. A few questions, however, made everything quite clear. Bibouker had discovered a safe and easy way to learn to ride a bicycle!

It was Bibouker who produced a delicacy most of us had met before, but incog.—that is to say, cat, cooked as rabbit. It wasn't bad, there was really very little difference, but somehow I lost my appetite for this dish when I discovered another cat gorging itself on a fresh corpse.

\* \* \* \* \* \*

Christmas came and went, not very different from any other day. We worked hard, building trenches and repairing roads, which called forth no little grousing from the English. That night we got extra wine, a few oranges, and rice prepared with chocolate with our supper. The *sous-officiers* congregated in a big room; but the soldiers and corporals, having no place to go, retired to their quarters where they sat in semi-darkness—quietly drinking. The volunteers added a new verse to their marching song:

> As we go working,
> Picks and shovels, on our way—Gor' blimee!
> You can hear the people shouting
> The bloody Legion works on Christmas Day.

## COFFEE, AND A RIOT

By this time the battalion had lost a good many, besides casualties. Some who had enlisted, just before the war, as Belgians, turned out to be German spies.

Stuart, Paul, a long lanky Southerner, and two or three other Americans had been *reformés* (discharged physically unfit) mostly on account of inflammatory rheumatism. The English had been transferred *en masse* to the British Army, and I found out later that most of them had applied for the Army Service Corps (Strawberry Jam Stealers) and wondered how they fared in that Paradise of military brigands, after four months' training in the Legion—or rather, how their new comrades fared, after their arrival.

Bill and Bert had gone to the aviation. Bill with his previous experience qualified at once as pilot. Bert's debut was typical. He climbed into the machine, had the controls explained to him, and started off just as Bill had done. Full speed ahead, up, and then down with a crash. After they had extracted him from the débris the officer in charge questioned him.

"What went wrong?"

"I don't know."

"You don't know! Haven't you ever been in a plane before?"

"No."

"What in God's holy name do you mean—starting off like that?"

"Well, I thought I might be able to fly."

They decided he had enough nerve to be worth training.

Then we lost Phil. It all started over a cup of coffee. Bibouker was ladling it out, and Bronstein, an English-American-Russian, was trying for a second cup, insisting he had had none. Bibouker waxed wroth and swore all Americans were cheats and liars. Given one other Arab, he said he could make the whole American section eat the dungheap in the yard. He called to a passing friend, an Arab from the machine gun section, to bear witness. Phil, who had been listening, stepped forward laughing and suggested that he and Bronstein take them on. Bibouker backed down, but the other Arab seemed eager, so the fight was on.

Phil generally packed a gun but he gave it to me at the start. The Arab pretended not to know this and to be nervous, and Phil held out his arms to show it wasn't on his hip. Whereupon,

## COFFEE, AND A RIOT

the Arab gripped him by the arms and butted him in the face. They both went down and came to grips, and Phil was gradually getting the best of it. They were fighting in a field covered with little piles of manure, and by this time a crowd had gathered. An Alsacian, a friend of the Arab, broke through the ring and cracked Phil over the head with a *bidon* (water bottle) full of wine. Figured out in physics, this meant a five-pound weight at the end of a four-foot lever, taking into consideration the length of the man's arm and the strap. Phil went down, and a general riot broke loose—our section against the machine gun outfit. An officer rushed in to stop it, calling on the sergeants to help him. *"A moi, les sergeants!"* He drew a gun, but before he could fire Thérisien, roaring, *"J' arrive, mon Lieutenant,"* hurled himself at the back of his knees and bowled him over. Finally the guard turned up and stopped the fight, but not before five Americans and six *Légionaires* had been knocked cold, and several others mildly marred. Both sides retired, growling at each other, and our billets were changed.

Phil was in a bad way, and growing worse daily. He thought it was a return of African black water fever, but it was hard to get proper treatment for this sort of thing. The doctor on duty was not impressed, and after painting the wound on his head with iodine, pronounced him fit for service.

I tried to beg, buy, or steal him some hot milk, but to no avail. The good samaritans slammed their doors in my face, in spite of my offers to pay. Two days later we moved up to the second line. The march finished him. He was taken to hospital, babbling with delirium, and died after three days of agony—tetanus.

The Alsacian was court-martialed, but acquitted on the ground that he was drunk at the time. Why shouldn't we get drunk? Goaded by criticism for having started the row, Bronstein walked over, followed by the section, and picked a fight with the Alsacian. In two minutes it was general, but the Alsacian was a marked man. While we kept up a milling battle with the others, every one of us concentrated on the Alsacian. When he went down it was all over. It is surprising how quickly hob-nailed Army boots can reduce a man's head to pulp.

Then the guard turned out, and we were all arrested. The major examined the case, and

## COFFEE, AND A RIOT

privately sympathized with us. But what could he do? There had been a row between the two sections, and a man had been killed. How could anyone tell who had done it? Anyway, he explained to our sergeants, putting us under arrest was as much to protect us as anything else. Most of the muleteers of the machine gun section carried knives, and in case another row started—?

## Chapter Five

## SCRAPS

MAY 1915. The train was teeming with Tommies, officers, W. A. A. C.s, and other feminine military organizations necessary in conducting a war, and I was a very blue spot of blue in all that khaki. With true *flegme brittanique*, I was discussed, but not spoken to.

"I say, old horse, whatever is he?"

"Don't know, must be a bloody Belgian."

"What's his rank?"

"Couldn't say, old bean, must be an officer, travelling first."

I was out of luck; the compartment was full of temporary gentlemen—Flying Corps, at that. I wondered what had happened to that finest type of man, the pre-war British officer. Had they all gone west at Mons?

Southampton at last, and I started aboard the leave boat. I was stopped at the gangplank by an M.E.O., who demanded my travel warrant. I explained I was not travelling under orders

## SCRAPS

but was a French soldier returning from leave. The British had apparently never heard of leave being granted, at least not to a private; and I instantly became a suspicious character, and was referred to the civilian passport control.

Why had I, a soldier in uniform, come to the civilian authorities? . . . Because the military police had sent me . . . . Then where was my passport, and visa? . . . I had neither . . . . Then I came under military jurisdiction.

Finally I was turned over to a military embarkation major. I explained the case, pointed out that if I did not catch that boat I would be twenty-four hours late; and twenty-four hours absence in time of war is desertion, the penalty for which is death, in the Foreign Legion. The major, a decent sort of chap, argued the matter for ten minutes through a curtain with an irate general who had apparently retired for the night, but to no avail. Whereupon the highly suspected spy was turned loose in the town and told to look up the French Consul next day.

The Consul was furious and gave me a letter stating that I had presented myself in plenty of time, papers in order, and that I was not to blame for the delay. This was fortunate, for

## TEN THOUSAND SHALL FALL

the British made amends by a very curt note which would have been about as helpful as a death warrant. I found out later. On arriving in France, I had to go back to the depot of the Legion, then situated at Orléans, and wait for the next draft before rejoining the regiment at the front.

Life at the depot was hell. I successfully resisted the offers of the doctors there to pronounce me physically unfit for a thousand francs, but gained the enmity of most of the depot draft by asking to leave for the front with the next reinforcements.

On board a troop train,
July 16, 1915.

Dear Gerald:

... We have been travelling all day and have changed trains four times. The carriage is getting dark. There is a jumble of sleeping men, sacks, rifles, cartridges, belts and haversacks strewn on the narrow benches. Very little talking, except for a drunken sergeant, and no singing. These aren't the gay, carefree men going to the front for the first time. Most of them have been there, as I have, during the long, dreary winter months, and have been sent back wounded or sick. We have been travelling sixteen hours, and as yet have not had a chance to fill our can-

*Conti,—dog fancier.*

*The Legion on the March, August, 1915.*

teens. A stop—everyone wakes—and a rush for the fountain. A struggle—"En voiture!"—and back we go to our wagons, without water. A few curses and a little grumbling, and silence again. But don't make a mistake. If these men don't shout and sing, they are none the less effective. And they are far more useful stone-walling material than the eager, imaginative, would-be bayonet-workmen of the green troops. . . .

. . . There is a fresh rumor, with some confirmation, that we are going to the Dardanelles. "We ain't got much money, but we do see life!" You don't know how glad I am to get away from that damned depot. At least I shall be among men. There is no one left but embusqué officers and little Jew tailors who have been more or less forced to join. Their one idea is to keep away from the front. They had to dress one by force, and all the time he kept yelling *"J'ai peur de partir!"* God, it must be awful not to have enough pride to conceal it if you are afraid!

I found the regiment at Plancher les Mines, near Belfort, due to a concentration of troops near the Alsacian border, as the powers-that-be were expecting an offensive in that direction.

\* \* \* \* \* \*

For a month we were in clover. Billets were beautifully clean and fairly comfortable, and the inhabitants more than friendly, and there were two or three *bistros* or inns. There was no work, but manoeuvres, route marches and reviews came thick and fast.

First and second *Etrangers,* eighth Zouaves, first Moroccan *Tirailleurs,* second Algerian *Tirailleurs,* colonial Artillery, and two squadrons of *Chasseurs d'Afrique.* Twenty-five thousand picked men—the Moroccan Division—to be reviewed by Leyautey.

Long columns of marching troops on the way to the field; *Légionaires* in the new sky-blue uniforms; zouaves and tirailleurs in khaki—great baggy trousers and red *chechia* (fezzes)—and the *Chasseurs d'Afrique* in pale blue *shakos* and dolmans.

The division forms three sides of a square. "Stack arms—stand at ease . . . . Attention!" Bugles and drums sound the *Garde à vous.* "*Rompez les faisceaux! Sacs aux dos!* . . . . A moment's pause . . . . "*Adroite alignement—fixe!*" Starting with the regiment on the right of the square, orders ripple down the line from one end of the division to the other. . . . "*Baionet-on!*" *(Baionettes au canon)** . . . . .

*Fix bayonets.

## SCRAPS

A flash of white steel in the sunlight. *"Présentez armes!"* The division looks like a wheatfield of bayonets.

A slim officer in general's uniform, followed by his staff, rode up to the entrance of the square, and the *clique*\* of the first Etranger crashed out the *Générale*. The drums and bugles of the other regiments took it up as he reached them. He tore along at full gallop with the figure and *élan* of a young cavalry officer. In spite of years of responsibility, he had kept his fire, but the keen hawk face was that of an old man.

He made the round of the regiments and came to a halt in the center of the square, and the massed bands played *Au Drapeau* and then the "Marseillaise."

I think most of us had a choky feeling. A day like this made up for a lot. A staff officer went down the line, informing the various captains that the general wished to speak to all those who had served with him in Africa. There is something of the Little Corporal in Leyautey: the cynical, hard-bitten *Légionaires* returned to the ranks, shoulders back and eyes shining.

\*Drums and bugles.

## TEN THOUSAND SHALL FALL

Then the march past began. For the first time we heard the march of the Legion played by a full band. The zouaves, Moroccans and Algerians filed past with their strange gliding swing, to the air *"Sidi Brahim."* Their way of sliding over the ground seemed to fit in with the combination of weird Algerian bagpipes *(nubas)* and bugles. The rumble of guns and caissons, the thunder of cavalry riding by at the charge. *Ca y est*—it was over!

\* \* \* \* \* \*

We were getting soft—good food and no work—so forced marches were the order of the day. The first was a little jaunt to the top of the *Balon de Surveillance* and back—fifty-seven kilometres with a climb of fifteen hundred feet. Before reentering the village, the *clique* went to the head of the column and the Legion marched in with their long, rolling swing as if they had just started. However, in spite of the efforts, to tame them down the men were in the pink of training, and fights and drunken brawls in the various *bistros* were becoming a nuisance.

I was sitting with Bob, the negro prize-fighter, in the most disreputable café in the place, when the door flew open and a little Italian *Légionaire* tore through the room, like a scared dog through a country village, and out the other side. A minute later, an enormous half-breed Algerian, his pock-marked face lit up like a Tibetan devil mask, and stark raving mad with cheap liquor, lurched through the door. He was followed by a huge Russian in similar condition. Lolling over the nearest table they questioned the little group of serious drinkers as to the whereabouts of Marius, evidently the late departed bar-room sprinter.

"Have you seen Marius?"

"No!"

"You lie! *Bande de salauds!*" (You swine!)

Whereupon, they each grabbed two empty bottles by the neck, broke the bottoms off against the table, and with these improvised glass daggers, blundered down the room slashing out impartially as they went.

Bob's reaction was immediate.

"Look here, boy! Ah seen this befo'. You do like me." And he promptly ducked under the table. I bumped heads with him in my eagerness to imitate. As soon as the roisterers had swept by, we were out and up; wrenched a leg apiece from the table, and stole after them.

## TEN THOUSAND SHALL FALL

Bob crowned one and I the other, and then the guard came.

Next day was pay day and the night was hell. The American section was on guard duty. Three or four *Légionaires* had determined to enter a house, and the women were hanging out of the top story, yelling. We arrived in time to see an attack worthy of a battlefield. The Legion Lotharios lined up across the street, bayonets fixed, rifles at the correct angle. As one man, they hurled themselves forward. Piercing shrieks from the women as the bayonets plunged into the door—then we fell upon them before they could wrench free.

Towards morning we were called out for the twenty-third time; but how to cram any more into the bursting jail was a problem. The sergeant of the guard, however, rose to the occasion. Placing the prisoners outside the door, he rapped out directions. We surrounded them with fixed bayonets. Throwing open the jail door, he ordered us to advance. As the points pricked them, the prisoners cursing and howling with fear fought their own way into the teeming clink.

Alan Seeger had a new crony, a gigantic Serb

## SCRAPS

called Hupmaja. He was a veteran of the last Balkan war and was probably a brigand before that. But he had abandoned brigandage for the law, and was studying in Paris when the war broke out. When he wasn't cleaning and crooning to his rifle, he was arguing with Alan.

In the heat of one of these discussions Alan called him an imbecile. Now he might have insulted his ancestors for ten generations, and Hupmaja would have grinned; but to insult his limited intelligence was striking too near home. With a roar the fight began; Alan sticking to the Marquess of Queensbury, and Hup using kill as catch can rules.

"Stick to out-fighting, Alan!"

"Don't let that Gorilla close with you!"

"Use your knee if he does!"

But in spite of all friendly advice they came to grips, and crashed to the ground—Alan underneath. The struggle went on but the Serb had it all his own way, and his thumbs crept towards the corners of Alan's eyes. A fight's a fight, but gouging is mutilation—so we kicked his thick head, and stopped it.

There were other troubles, besides drinking. The first grenades had appeared—cranky things made by women munition workers. They were guaranteed to go off in seven seconds, but occasionally exploding in three, and there were several tragedies during practice. But it was left to a Corsican sergeant to use them for his own private grudge. Hate is never far from love. Torrelli had been thrown down by his girl, and his hot blood demanded revenge. He pranced up to her house with a neat paper package under his arm, and tried to inveigle her to come out. The gist of it all was to let bygones be bygones but he wanted to make her a parting present. His expression, or perhaps her intuition, warned her something was wrong. Instead of coming forward to take the package, she questioned him through the half-closed door. The more he urged, the more distantly curious she became. The argument ended abruptly—as the present exploded. Marie was considerably shaken. Torrelli disappeared in a fine red mist.

\* \* \* \* \* \*

Alsace was a great disappointment. The *"Quand Même"* and "Little Bird from France" stuff was useful as propaganda, but we hadn't been there a day before we discovered it was eye-wash—or, shall we say, banana oil! It

## SCRAPS

seemed to me that most of the French Alsacians must have cleared out after 1870. The present population is neither anti German nor pro French; they simply want to be an independent state, like Switzerland or Luxembourg. They were anti Boche for good reasons, but principally, because they are *always* "agin the government." After I had been there a week, I was convinced they would prove as much of a stumbling block in the Chambre as they had in the Reichstag. The cafés were amusing. French was evidently the patriotic tongue of the moment. It was comic to watch the worthy Burghers come in, raise their hats and solemnly greet the gathering: *"Ponchour dout le monde-Zalut, la gompagnie!"* Their French went no further, but honor was satisfied—and with a sigh of relief they would lapse into guttural German.

*Chapter Six*

## BATTLE OF CHAMPAGNE

The 2nd Etrangers disentrained at St. Hilaire the night of Sept. 15th. The road was blocked with regiments. I had never seen so many men. At dawn we moved on, and even as we moved, troops, by this time banked up behind us, took our place. Regiments, brigades, divisions,—Line, Chasseurs Alpins, Zouaves, Tirailleurs, Colonial Infantry, what next! Guns, field guns, Howitzers, siege batteries, endless ammunition trains—then cavalry. Our hopes ran high—it was the big offensive—open warfare—Berlin! Still the blue columns rolled on—picked men, shock troops—the lance head of the army. There must be a big show coming and, as if in confirmation, the German guns began a sullen systematic shelling. We camped in the park of the *Château* at Suippes and lost touch with the shifting horde in the intensity of our own preparations. Every day officers went up into line to learn the trenches and returning explained

## BATTLE OF CHAMPAGNE

with plans scratched on the ground. A. was our first line, B., C. and D. evacuation trenches, and God help the man who was caught in one of these without a wound. Specialists were trained. Grenadiers with the new contact grenades, whose business it was to put the machine guns out; *Nettoyeurs des Tranchées* with wicked looking trench daggers, to mop up after the first wave had swept over—there was to be no repetition of Arras. And still more troops and guns rolled up.

Our preparatory bombardment began. God what a prelude! It crashed out on a split second, and for three days thundered relentlessly on. In the face of this, how childish our new gas masks and steel helmets. . . .

"Hey, feller, tomorrow's the big day!"

"Yeh—Thérisien just told me."

"Did he tell you we're not going to lead off, after all?"

"Yep—We've got the dirtiest job of all. The Colonial Infantry's going over first. We pass 'em, and take over just where the hardest fighting begins, and when we're shot to pieces the Zouaves carry on through the gap."

"Sounds pleasant!" Then Denny's voice

dropped, as he sheepishly handed me a bit of paper. "That's my sister's address, Dave, just in case . . . . Will you write?"

"Sure. Here's my brother's."

Evening came—everything was ready. Huddled around the dying fires we *bleus* were trying to hide our stage-fright, and the *anciens* were singing the traditional songs of the Legion—and over everything the increasing roar of the guns.

"*Rassemblement! Couvrez sur deux!*"

"We're for it now, Denny."

"Yes, feller, but what an experience!"

At 12 sharp we started for the line in column of twos. As we got clear of the woods we could hear troops marching on all sides. Occasionally we got fleeting glimpses of them as the moon came out of the clouds. The shells were beginning to burst around us now, but we were comparatively safe in the shelter of a *boyeau*.*

Suddenly we came out into the street of a little village. This was Souain, and at that moment no healthy spot. Two of our batteries were in the ruins and the whole place was lit up by the flash of the guns. The German guns were searching for them, and the noise of crashing

*Communication trench.

## BATTLE OF CHAMPAGNE

shells and tumbling masonry was infernal. As we passed the door of a huge barn I saw an Artillery man, hands in pockets, legs wide apart, grinning from ear to ear. He made some remark about it being a bit showery. Another flash—Abracadabra! His goblin figure disappeared.

We plunged into another *boyeau* and finally reached the second line, where in spite of a fine rain and the bombardment we slept like logs. At dawn we were up watching the effect of our shells. They were bursting like ocean breakers on the first and second German line, following each other so fast that they howled like a wind overhead.

On account of poor visibility, zero hour was postponed till nine. At nine sharp the order was passed *"Sacs aux dos,"* and we started to the first line, our section in front with Rosé leading. We came to a place where the *boyeau* was cut by a road. Beside us a masked battery had opened up and was working full blast. The Germans were hunting for it and had just got the range. They were dropping big shells at the point of crossing, and were sweeping it with machine guns.

TEN THOUSAND SHALL FALL

*Commandant* Rosé climbed out onto the road, looked coolly about him, and walked across with his cane on his arm. I held my breath and plunged after him. Those of us who got across were surprised to find ourselves still alive.

At a fork in the *boyeau* we learned that the Colonial Infantry had led off; already some of the wounded were streaming back. I was so interested in a Colonial with the tops of four fingers shot off that I lost contact with the rest of the section, and found myself with the men behind me, including Lieutenant Pelozza, cut off from the rest.

We blundered into the first line trench as a section of Colonials was about to go over. Out in front of the trench a *commandant majeur* (doctor with the grade of major) was walking up and down. There he was, bullets and shrapnel whistling all about him, swinging his stick as he calmly directed the stretcher bearers. Seeing us he hailed Lieutenant Pelozza. *"Hey, que faites vous là!"* ("What are you doing there?") Pelozza explained that we had lost our regiment, etc. He was bothered for a moment, and then his face cleared. *"Vous allez tous dans la même direction. Vous n'avez qu'à foutre le camp avec*

## BATTLE OF CHAMPAGNE

*les autres."* (You are all going in the same direction, you'd better jump off with the rest.)

Once out of the communication trench we lost all awe of the bullets which were spatting about us and started across the level ground. A roar of rage from Captain Petaud, on the left, called us back: "What the HELL are you doing out there!" And rejoining the regiment, we meekly waited our turn.

Prisoners began to filter in. Poor devils, half crazed from the effects of the bombardment, they offered us everything they had, from watches to water bottles. Four of them were bearing a Colonial captain on a stretcher. He saw the green 2's on our collars, and raising himself cried, *"Vive la Légion!"*—Then he fell back exhausted, the blood welling from a jagged hole in his chest.

We fixed bayonets. Commandant Rosé jumped out ahead—*"En Avant"* we were off. We crossed their front line at a quick walk, and for the first time got some idea of the effect of our bombardment. Nothing was left but a series of mounds and holes with half-buried men, machine guns, and barbed wire entanglements—here and there a dead Colonial hanging on them.

## TEN THOUSAND SHALL FALL

We began to lose men by rifle and machine gun fire, as well as shrapnel. A halt to get the men in hand again, and I had a chance to look around. Behind me in every direction came heavy columns of blue-clad Infantry. Regiment after regiment surged over the hill—an overwhelming flood of blue. "Hey! Look at the cavalry!" Sure enough, we could see columns of horsemen. As they came broadside to us we noticed the strange formation in which they were riding—six men by twos—then a gap—then six more. Suddenly we realized they were not cavalry but batteries following up the Infantry. Five minutes later they came galloping into the flat sort of valley where we were waiting. The boches caught sight of both the guns and us at the same moment. The result was a veritable hail of 4.2 inch shrapnel and the famous German 105" shell.

We lay flat with our sacks hunched on our shoulders and watched the guns come into action. A contact shell hit the lead team of one gun and "messed 'em up considerable." In a flash the wheel driver was at the horses' heads calming them, the gunners had cut loose the quivering mass of horses and men, and what was

## BATTLE OF CHAMPAGNE

left of the team was on its way again, the driver swinging into his saddle at the trot. A minute later the battery was in action front and had fired its first salvo.

A shell burst just above us and the man on my left gave a little moan. The Corporal on my right buried his face in his hands squeaking like a snared rabbit, and my rifle burned my hands. There was no doubt about the other man—he was through; the Corporal was weeping in such a high falsetto we thought he was fooling, but when we pulled his hands down from his face we found it split open like a ripe melon. In the meantime, I had troubles of my own; the same shrapnel had smashed my rifle so I had to look around for another. It was not difficult to find one as men were dropping all around and there was one continuous yell for *brancardiers* (stretcher bearers). According to orders they only brought in men of their own regiment; it looked cruel to see them pass a man with his whole side torn out to pick up another slightly wounded, but it saved lives in the long run.

Things were becoming a little too warm in that part of the world so we were ordered to occupy a German position, the "Angelheartshooting trench." Here, however, in spite of the pleasing name things were even worse. They had the range down to an inch, and were only waiting to make sure it was occupied before plastering it with heavy contact shells. A sickening crash, the stench of hot acrid gas—the pelting of rocks sand and clods of earth, and finally the shrieks of the wounded. Two hours of this, and at last the order to advance once more. This meant climbing out, assembling, and calling the roll, under the same murderous fire.

The first, second and third sections fell in and numbered off; only five men and a sergeant of the fourth appeared. Captain Petaud waited patiently for a bit but finally shouted to the sergeant, "Come along, Malvoisin! Where is the rest of your section?" Malvoisin gave a dry chuckle, "We're all here, Captain." Petaud never turned a hair. "Oh, I see. It's like that." And he gave the order to advance. They started shelling us with shrapnel as soon as we moved, but anything was better than being wiped out like ants in that ditch.

A cyclist came up with a message. Colonel Le Compte Denny had been wounded and Major Rosé was to command the regiment. Petaud

## BATTLE OF CHAMPAGNE

took over the battalion, and Lieutenant Hallouette, or "Jo Jo, the Dog-Faced-Boy," as we called him, took our company. He had been a reserve officer, but was considered too old for active service when the war broke out, so he resigned his commission and enlisted in the Legion. Within a year he had won the *Médaille Militaire* and was back in his old rank of lieutenant through sheer efficiency and courage. He was the finest shot in the regiment, and could outlast the best men in his company on the march. He carried a full sack and spurned his horse as an example to the men.

The battalion advanced in open order and, just at dusk, dug in about two hundred yards back of the Ferme de Navarin. The ground was strewn with little patches of newly turned earth covered with straw, and the first man to step on one went up with a loud bang—field mines.

Denny and I were *copins de combat* (battle side-kicks) so we dug in together. As we flopped down, our hearts stopped: we were bang in the middle of one of those sinister patches of straw! Fortunately it was a dud, so we shifted and went to ground.

Our battalion had advanced too far and was

enfiladed on the left flank, so moved back to a little ridge some twenty-five yards to the rear.

The battalion on the right had taken the Ferme de Navarin but our gunners didn't know it and our barrage stuck fast, just in front of the farm. The German barrage was some twenty yards back of the farm, so the battalion was boxed. Fritz discovered their predicament first, and shortened his range . . . .

Meantime, we were consolidating our position on the ridge. The Germans turned everything they had on us—shrapnel, marmites (H-E shell), aerial torpedoes, and machine guns. It was raining hard by now—it always rained when the allies attacked—so much so, that we began to think there was something in the "Gott mit uns" slogan. As fast as we dug the holes filled with water.

About midnight chaos broke out in the Ferme de Navarin. Wild firing, then the panic-stricken bleating of the battalion holding it, guttural German cheers, and clear-cut commands of French officers trying to rally their men, (it was a line battalion made up entirely of the young class of 1916). The Boches had

"Shirt reading" between attacks, Champagne, September, 1916.

"*And some dig deeper in the chalk.*"

## BATTLE OF CHAMPAGNE

counter attacked and the kids had broken and scattered.

Suddenly a bugle cut clear and calm through all the noise and confusion—first the regimental call of the Legion, then the rally.

The German shouting stopped. There was a half-hearted cheer from the young troops. The Legion went mad. Every man sprang to his feet and whipped out his bayonet— The bugle began again—clear and inviting it sounded the charge. This was too much! Low growls ran down the line— We started forward with the long swinging *pas de charge*. The officers ran out in front, beating us back with the flat of their sabres.

"Stay where you are! Don't fire! We must wait till they are driven back to us and then counter attack."

Discipline held—the Legion subsided and waited with grim expectancy. Now the bugler had passed to the double time of the charge! The kids pulled themselves together and fairly hustled the Germans out of the farm.

Bugle calls are forbidden in time of war, to avoid traps. When the confusion started Petaud was visiting the defenders of the farm, followed by the regimental bugler. Sizing up the situation, he immediately ordered the bugler to sound the rally and charge—it did the trick.

All the day of the 26th was spent in consolidating our position under heavy shell fire. Alan described it in his poem "Maktoob."

> "When, not to hear, some try to talk
> And some to clean their guns, or sing,
> And some dig deeper in the chalk—
> I look upon my ring."

Sept. 27th. Waguenenestre brought mail last night. Got six letters. Too dark to see. Wondered if I'd be killed before I could read 'em. Waked by knapsack landing on me. Morlae's. Roused Ole and Denny and went to investigate. Found same shell buried him alive. Got him out just in time—gasping like fish. Went to sleep again. Attack still going forward. Moved back to reform with Bat. D. Old German trench. Range down pat. Not so good. Raining again. Kitchens came right up into line—Hot food!

\* \* \* \* \* \*

Orders! We were to take the Bois de Sabots, on the right of the line, but had to cross the

## BATTLE OF CHAMPAGNE

whole field of battle to get into position to attack. We started off by sections in column of twos, four abreast at distances of fifty yards. The Germans spotted us and turned everything loose, but the columns pushed on. Shells burst full in the middle of sections, annihilating the center. The remaining men picked themselves up and joined sections to their right or left; the march continued.

Horrible apparitions crawled out of shell holes and looked at us as we went by. A thing with no face—only four caverns in a red mask, where eyes, nose and mouth had been—mooed and gibbered at us as it heard the clink of accoutrements passing. Some strong-minded humanitarian put a bullet into it as we filed by.

We reached a wood. It was like a scene from the underworld—ghostly columns picking their way through shell-torn trees in the smoke and fog of high explosives. A shell burst in the section on the right—it looked like a football scrimmage writhing in agony—a swirl of men and smoke. Shells cracked over our heads—shells tore up the ground in front of us. We took the last gap at the run.

All that were left of us joined the remnants

of three previous attacks. We crouched at the edge of the Bois de Sabots and peered through the underbrush. Oh Christ . . . . Two battalions of the Legion and one of *Chasseurs Alpins* were stretched out in skirmish order in front of the German barbed wire. The alignment was perfect—the men were dead.

We felt pretty sober till Ole Nielson began to sing "Ragtime Cowboy Joe." The section took it up with a roar, convulsed with mirth at the line. "No one but a lunatic would start a war." The other *Légionaires* grinned, but the *Chasseurs Alpins* looked at each other in horror, convinced we had gone mad.

"*Quatre hommes de bonne volontée!*" Commandant Rosé wriggled forward with them to reconnoiter. The place was stiff with machine guns and the barbed wire was not touched. A brief report to the General, demanding guns to blow a way through the wire—then we waited. Rosé had nerve. Just given command of the regiment, and his first act of initiative was to refuse to order a hopeless attack. He could have covered himself with glory while directing it in safety, from the rear. God, what a soldier he was!

## BATTLE OF CHAMPAGNE

Sept. 29th. Back last night where we started from. Repeated whole bloody performance today. Dug in. Shot up by our own guns again. Bois de Sabots outflanked and taken. Few losses.

Sept. 30th. Spent night converting German positions. Prying roof off dog kennel, needed planks. Out bounced Jo Jo, the dog faced boy.

Sept. 31st. Still digging, cleaning out Germ. dugouts. Found amusing p. c. to Germ. from girl—

"The troops on the eastern front are performing miracles of bravery and strategy. Why don't you advance? Do you know what people are saying in Berlin? 'In the east is an army of brave men. In the west are the village firemen.'"

Wonder how Fritz laughed off retreat. Fred found jar gun grease in dugout. Started to clean rifle—turned out to be honey. Better and better, said Alice.

Oct. 1st. Relieved last night. 30 Kiloms. to rear for rest. Everyone dead beat. 50 min. march. 10 min. rest. Dropped in our tracks. Had to be kicked awake. Reformed with remains 1st and 2nd Etrangers—one regiment.

## TEN THOUSAND SHALL FALL

Oct. 6th. Back to line yesterday. In immediate reserve today. Lost heavily . . . .

The work of consolidating the line began, grabbing off sectors still held by the Germans to round out the position, and burying the dead —simple enough once you know the trick. We would dig a hole beside the man and roll him in. As time was short, the holes were shallow. Men take strange positions in death. They did not always fit the grave, and some one would stand on the arms and legs, to keep them down while the others shovelled furiously. But when they have been dead a day or so, they are like enormous dolls with limbs worked by elastics. In some cases the burial party miscalculated the amount of earth needed to hold them down, and as the man standing on the corpse stepped aside, an arm or leg would slowly rise through the loose sand and earth, in mute protest.

\* \* \* \* \* \*

Oct. 19th, 1916.

"Dear Gerald:

I'm not going to write you a word about the battle . . . but I managed to snap some photos from time to time, and if they come out, I'll send you some prints . . . . . . One thing bores me like hell. We were go-

## BATTLE OF CHAMPAGNE

ing to work Indian file. A shell burst near us, and my friend, Fred, who was walking just ahead of me, gave a funny little squeak and fell back into my arms, fighting for breath and clutching at his side. There was another man scratched, and screaming like a stallion; as the stretcher men were around him, I picked Fred up and carried him down to the *poste de secours*. The shells were getting thicker and I was making the best time I could, so you can imagine my rage when I discovered he was still hanging onto his rifle. At the dressing station we found it was only a broken rib. Thank God it hadn't penetrated his lung . . ."

\* \* \* \* \* \*

The Legion had been so cut to pieces that the Powers That Be had almost decided to send it back to Africa. The volunteers were given the alternative, however, of going into a French regiment. Rosé called us together. "You're leaving the Foreign Legion—for God's sake don't go and spread the usual lies about it. We're not all cutthroats, perverts and sneak thieves. We're men who have had troubles of our own. We're a hard fighting regiment of professional soldiers, and we've won a glorious name. Don't go and smirch it! You've come up to standard—I'm sorry to lose you. Good luck!"

"Jo Jo" shook hands with me twice, and said

something I'm prouder of than any of my decorations—and I never even thought he had noticed me.... And we marched down to join our new regiment—the 170th Infantry—*"les Hirondelles de la Mort."*

*Chapter Seven*

## WE LEAVE AND RELIEVE THE LEGION

Out of the frying pan into the fire—Another attacking division! Thirty-two kilometres down—thirty-two kilometres back, the next day. By irony of fate, the 170th relieved the Legion. No rest for the wicked.

Then began the long drawn-out business of consolidating the ground taken in the advance; not very startling to read about in the *communiqués*. It was a dreary stretch—a blur of cold misery and overwork and mud. The nights were the worst. Two hours guard or outpost duty with eyes and ears strained—two hours' work—carrying enormous logs, rolls of barbed wire, stakes and *gabions* through tortuous mud-filled *boyeaux,* driving posts and stringing barbed wire outside the lines, filling sand bags and repairing trenches demolished during the day—then towards morning the long tramp to

## TEN THOUSAND SHALL FALL

the kitchens to bring up food for the next day—and at dawn everyone standing to arms.

One of our listening posts was only eight yards from a German outpost. The parapet was made of German and French dead, and the shallow communication trench leading to it was strewn with Germans. The ground above the trench was swept by machine gun fire day and night so that the relieving guard scuttled along it bent almost double—no time to throw the corpses over the side. A huge Prussian grenadier halfway along it we dubbed "Croaking Conrad" for if one stepped on his middle he still uttered a guttural frog-like croak.

In the post we sat, slept, even ate, sitting on corpses. But the night we were relieved came my breaking point. In the narrow entrance one of the relief bumped me and I lost my balance. I grabbed the parapet behind me to save myself from falling, and was almost sick as I felt a face come away under my hand. For days everything I ate or touched smelled of putrid flesh.

The Germans had advanced a machine gun post some twenty yards beyond their lines; very annoying to us. Seven of us climbed over, picked our way through the wire and began the

## WE LEAVE

usual business—wriggling through mud and over corpses, a rocket—stop, darkness—we scuttled forward. Our orders were to throw two bombs apiece and then get back as best we could. A black mound loomed up—a whispered command and fourteen grenades were hurled in rapid succession, wrecking the gun. Instantly, machine guns in the German line began to rake the spot.

All the way out I had been doing some hard thinking. *"Sauve qui peut,"* all very well—but where? Lie down till it blew over? Yeh, and be mopped up on the ground—not enough cover for a rabbit. Head straight back? Forty yards, and you can't beat a bullet. I ran parallel to the German lines till out of the zone of cross fire, and then cut back to our own lines. Three lay down and three raced bullets. I got home.

The Germans were strafing us more every day. They would begin at one end of a regimental front, hammer their way along it, let up for half an hour, and then begin again. At this time Fritz started the retarded fuse shells. We heard the dull thuds of the departure, the menacing crescendo whistle, then four more dull thuds. For a moment we thought they were duds, and cheered hilariously from sheer relief. A second later four muffled explosions, and cubic yards of earth, rock and chalk were hurled into the air. This was something new and nasty!

\* \* \* \* \* \*

I heard the swish and howl of a shell, and ducked behind a traverse. Sudden blackness—and I was struggling desperately for light and air under an avalanche of earth and sand bags. It seemed hours—but it could only have been seconds—before they cleared my head and dug me out. I looked around groggily, my knees trembling, on the verge of horrors. Did the sergeant tell me to go down to the dressing station, to sit down and think over my narrow escape and work myself up into a state of shell shock? He did not. The first thing I heard was a curse and a roar: "You holy bit of blood sausage! Don't you know there are others buried alive, too? Grab a tool and help dig them out. Make it snappy!" He took control of my mind before I had time to realize the shock, and directed it along normal channels. As I tore around the other traverse where the men were buried, I saw a pick and a shovel. Even as I ran, my mind decided the question which to take. Buried men—might kill them with a pick—

*One of a million.*

"A little home cooking."—Hoffeker, Dugan Rocle, Ganz (all killed).

## WE LEAVE

better take the shovel. Snatching it up in my stride I got to work.

Next morning the mist cleared suddenly, as it had a habit of doing at the front, and out beyond their wire was a German working party. I flung my rifle to my shoulder, closing my left eye—blank. What the .... ? I rubbed my eye and tried again—still nothing. That shell had made trouble after all .... Later, the oculist told me that it was due to the concussion. No chance of the aviation now—but after all I had one eye left. In any other army, I would probably have been coddled into a case of shell shock. This being the French Army, I learned to shoot from my left shoulder.

The matter was closed.

\* \* \* \* \* \*

Dec. 5, 1915.

" . . . . . . They have stuck me in the *peloton des éléves sous-offs* for 20 days hard, so it looks as if I won't ever get my four days home. Good Lord, they work us hard! Yesterday they had a little endurance race with our equipment and rifles, I didn't shine. And like the damphool I was my cartridge pouches were full. All the others had emptied theirs moons ago. Never

## TEN THOUSAND SHALL FALL

again! I have now arrived at the magnificent state of *Soldat première classe*—a distinction, but not a grade. I am entitled to wear one black stripe on my arm, but up to the present have been too lazy to sew it on. Hence earning a reputation of having a magnificent indifference for all military grades and honors. . . . . .

. . . . . . Just at present, I'm leading one hell of a life—neither fish nor fowl nor good red herring. We are *en repos*, waiting and getting ready for the dance this spring. If you want to know what sort of life it is, read Kipling's 'Gentlemen Rankers.' Almost all my friends have been wounded or have passed into the aviation. I can't, on account of my right eye. Well, Gerald, if I don't get it this spring, you had better stick close to me all your life, for I bear a charmed life. They have put me into the 'Chucka de bombsky' squad (Grenadiers); that means that we lead off the attack and try to put the machine guns and crews out before they can get the second wave which follows us. It has its advantages, though. We don't have to carry a sack in action, and there is talk of taking our rifles away and giving us automatic pistols. As I've packed an automatic right through the war, plus fifty rounds, it will relieve me of the damned old blunderbuss and the 250 rounds of rifle ammunition. In spite of what we know is coming, most of us are looking forward to it. Anything but this inactive life away from the front, and at the same time far from civilization. . . . . .

This letter is getting so long that I already have grave doubts if the censors will let it by, so I think I

## WE LEAVE

will ring off. Don't be uneasy about the spring. I've got the same hunch I've had since the beginning that I will get by without a scratch.
        In haste,
          Affec.,
                      Ding."

*Chapter Eight*

## VERDUN—SHOCK TROOPS

As fate would have it, the doctor chose the 17th February to innoculate us against typhoid. All morning, long lines of men seeped into the infirmary. Some fainted as they came in sight of the white-aproned doctor and his aides, wiping the needles, jabbing, and then wiping again. One of the aides was dealing out aspirin tablets as the victims went out, checking off the names and droning *"un jour exempt d'éxércise,"* in a sing-song voice, after each name. That night, the men moaned and tossed restlessly in the hayloft where we were quartered.

About midnight a new element of unrest: towards the northeast, the intermittent rumble of guns suddenly quickened and increased to concert pitch and volume. Even those who had been sleeping heavily stirred in their sleep, and some of the more wakeful lit candles and cigarettes, muttering to themselves, *"Ca chauffe la bàs. Pourvu que nous ne sommes pas appellés*

## VERDUN—SHOCK TROOPS

*demain."* ("It's warming up over there. Hope we are not called tomorrow.")

The division was supposed to be resting and training for the spring offensive, but an attacking division never knows . . . . We were offensive shock troops, but likely as not to be hurled into the line at any moment, to stop a gap. What we did know was that, once in, we were never withdrawn from a show till we had lost three quarters of our effectives.

At four o'clock came a shout from the farmyard below. *"Allons là haut! Tous le monde en bàs! Faites les sacs. On part à six heures."* ("Come on, everybody on deck! Make up the sacks. We leave at six.") Instantly everything was in a turmoil.

Candles were lighted and men groped feverishly in the straw for lost possessions and crammed them into their bursting knapsacks. Every few minutes a corporal would appear, followed by two men carrying half a pup-tent filled with things to be distributed: extra cartridges, emergency rations, first-aid kits, and last of all the squad cooking kettles. Finally the man of the day appeared with the coffee, which he poured into our outstretched cups. Too hot to drink! We set them in the straw to cool, where most of them were promptly upset. The general confusion was increased by shouts from below—*"Allez, allez! Grouillez-vous! Tout le monde en bàs! Les autos vont venir à six heures!"* ("Come on, make it snappy! Everybody down! The trucks are coming at six!")

By now most of us were in the farmyard. Squad after squad stacked rifles and sacks and waited. There were low mutterings. *"Les autos"*—not so good. That meant a particular sort of perpendicular hell when we got there—we only rode up to the show when a specially hot corner was reserved for us. No wonder the motor trucks were called "slaughtermobiles."

By 6:30 the big grey Renaults, Fiats, Whites and Saurers began to roll into the village, and company after company piled aboard, wincing as they put on their sacks. The innoculation was playing havoc with us. Spirits revived though with the dawn and we began to sing, bellowing forth outrageous ribald songs as the trucks rolled through half-wakened villages. We passed peasant girls in *sabots* coming from the bakery with the family loaves clasped under their arms, yawning as they walked—they

## VERDUN—SHOCK TROOPS

scarcely looked up, however, as the troops thundered by. The war had been going on for eighteen months now.

It began to snow and then freeze, and snow again. The trucks skidded from the high-crowned roads; soon the three leading ones were in the ditch and the road was blocked. No luck —we were ordered to get out.

"*Allons! Rassemblement! Couvrez sur deux! Sacs aux dos! En avant par quatres!*" And the heavy, grey-blue column got under way, shuffling precariously along the icy road. Every few yards someone slipped and fell. Nobody laughed. It's no joke to go down with a hundred pounds of sharp-edged equipment on your shoulders, particularly after an innoculation. The stumbling, slipping column plodded on and on. . . .

Three o'clock, and a halt is called in a village. We begin to speculate on the chances of soup, and staying there for the night. "*Formez les faisceaux! Sacs à terre.*" Ah, that's better. But hopes are dashed as an order trickles down from the head of the column: "Don't let them undo their sacks or break ranks." Sure enough, a cyclist comes up to the colonel with an envelope. *"Sacs aux dos! En avant par quatres!"* And the weary column gets under way once more. Heads down and shoulders hunched, eyes glued to the feet of the man in front—we stumble after them, hypnotized . . . .

Four o'clock, and it begins to snow again. The guns grow more and more insistent and the roar is numbing. Suddenly, freakish shapes loom up on the road ahead. They crowd to one side as the column slouches by: old men in queer, heterogeneous apparel—women pushing baby carriages, piled high with household possessions over and above the wailing occupant.

Terror-stricken, dumb, they drift by like startled ghosts; their wide eyes scarcely see the troops. Women, half pushed, half dragged along, calling for killed or missing babies. Lost children struggling to keep up with forced, uneven steps, moaning pitifully for dead parents! "Where do you come from? What's going on?" we shout in passing. But the only answer is a murmur—"The big shells—oh, the big shells!"

We know we are going to Verdun. But it conveys little, except that it has always been a quiet *secteur*. On we go through the night. At ten, half an hour's halt to eat bread, sardines,

## VERDUN—SHOCK TROOPS

cheese. Still snowing, and the going more and more treacherous. The hours string out till there seems no end to this nightmare of a march. The guns are near, now. Occasionally men cock their heads to one side, persuaded they hear the whistle of a shell, but as yet it's only the wind in the telegraph wires.

Five o'clock. Fort de la Sartelle, the first of the group around Verdun. Our march is over. We are herded in and flop on the stone floor half an inch deep in water. Who cares—we may sleep! We have come sixty-five kilometres in nineteen hours' forced marching over ice-coated roads, but no one cares, except the general, who is awaiting fresh troops.

Two hours later, seven o'clock, and the column is under way again. We skirt the city and make for a wood, in which to hide from enemy aircraft while waiting for definite orders. Vain hope. A high-pitched thrum in the air; overhead a French observation plane tries desperately to escape some fourteen German scouts. The moment they spot us they turn back, and flying back and forth over the road proceed to bomb us. A short command, and we scatter over the fields. The planes disappear, whistles blow, and

## TEN THOUSAND SHALL FALL

ten minutes later the regiment is on the march again. The seeming loose discipline, for which French troops are criticised, has one advantage—it makes large bodies of men more flexible.

Nervous business waiting for orders under fire, especially in the woods. We can see nothing and the crash of explosion echoes and re-echoes, so that every shell seems to have dropped within ten yards of us. A series of dull thuds as the shells leave the guns—boooomp, boooomp, boomp. Then a crescendo wail—phoo-o-o, phoo-o-o, pho-o-o-o. Brammmm! A black column of smoke—shrieks from the wounded—and calls for stretcher bearers. A quarter of an hour later a pathetic little *cortège* starts to the rear—four men carrying a blood-stained canvas trough, in which lies a quivering, moaning mass of mangled flesh, in dirty clothes and blood-soaked bandages. A heroic bid on the part of pigmies for a comrade's life, but the odds are on his bleeding to death or the whole *cortège* being wiped out on the way.

Our nerves have readjusted themselves to the noise, now. Mercifully, after several hours' bombardment, high explosives act like a soporific.

Night falls and a move is ordered. Ghostly

## VERDUN—SHOCK TROOPS

columns leave the wood and advance along the road. Sibilant orders run down the lines: "You are in sight and perhaps in hearing of the enemy. No smoking. No talking. Keep your bayonet scabbards from clanking, and try to keep your feet from sucking in the mud."

The shelling has ceased for the moment, and the silence of the regiment is almost uncanny. Presently, the leading company tops a hill, and a ripple of laughter floats back to us. We have been pussy-footing it along as if the Boches were just around the corner, and there, in the valley ahead, the other regiment of our brigade is encamped and cheerful pandemonium reigns. Tents are pitched and candles burn brightly. Officers shriek at the top of their lungs for companies and sections, and companies and sections call for their soup kitchens, and shells crash and whine in the midst of it all. *"Troisieme compagnie. Troisieme compagnie." "Hch! la cuisine du quatrième!" "Premiere section à la soupe." "Hep, la bàs! Etcindres ces bougies."* Fo-o-o-o-e-e-! Crash! Etc.

An hour later we have had soup and are off. The division is split up between two army corps. The brigade is split, even the battalions of our regiment are lent out right and left. The Boches have attacked unexpectedly and in force. They have taken the first and second lines. Vaux still holds out but Douaumont has fallen. Rumors fly: there has been treachery—the general in command has been shot—two regiments were marched by a *poiteau d'éxécution,* with a general's *képi* on it, as proof.

Now the real work begins. The counter attack has driven the Boches back, and surrounded Douaumont, but it is still held by a battalion of Brandenburgers. An hour's march in the heavy mud and slush, fifteen minutes to marshal the regiment into position, and the whistles shrill out for the charge. The night is stabbed by weird streaks of light as machine guns in the fort open up, and part of the advancing line crumples like burnt paper. But with the snarl of a wounded leopard, the rest dash on and clear the outer ramparts.

Position after position is taken, and the various machine gun crews are wiped out. No quarter is expected or given. A machine gun spits, three or four grenades snap, a rush, a scuffle, thuds and curses, and the attackers go on. As the fort is cleared, the inevitable happens—at-

## VERDUN—SHOCK TROOPS

tacking squads fire into each other. The Brandenburgers fight to the last man; there is no question of prisoners. Finally the job is done. The regiments left and right send troops to take over the fort and the attackers withdraw to lick their wounds.

Dawn finds us back in the same woods, once more in the position of immediate reserves, for we are still considered fresh troops, and, indeed, we are now thoroughly in our stride.

I wander down the hill to visit Billy Dugan, in the second company. Pipe in mouth and hands in pocket, I register coolness. As I arrive, three or four big shells shake the earth fifty yards off, and give me a cue.

"What are you guys doing? Dumping bricks? I wish you'd quit it. You've spoiled my beauty sleep."

However, in relaxing my jaw to speak, my outraged nerves rebel and the pipe wobbles like a crazy pendulum.

"That? Oh, they're just a few late New Year's presents from Fritz. But, say, old man, would you mind smoking a cigarette for a while? That pipe of yours makes us dizzy."

## TEN THOUSAND SHALL FALL

An ominous whistling rush cuts all conversation as we flop. A 210" bursts slap in the middle of a section, sending men hurtling into the air, sacks on backs, rifles still grasped in their hands. We look at each other, awe-struck. *"C'était la troisième de la quatrième."* Then as our nerves relax, *"Tu as vu la drôle de gueule Gaillard faisait?"* (Did you see what a funny face Gaillard pulled?) Callous, perhaps, but if we let ourselves go after everything of this sort we would be demoralized in a day. As it is, we save our sympathy for the wounded, and rush to help.

Food is short, but rumors are plentiful. *Agents de liaison* pass with news of the other regiment—strange clipped accounts that somehow tell the whole story. "You should see the 174th. They got theirs. There'll be plenty of extra *pinard* for everyone, when they do draw it again. And as for stripes, we'll be holy zebras—if we get through this show. Look you—a quarter-master sergeant led back all that was left of two companies and a *sous-lieutenant* is commanding a battalion."

"Perhaps—but the new draft from the depot

## VERDUN—SHOCK TROOPS

will have too many animals with sardines on their forelegs."*

"The only way to get promotion is to be wounded and go to the depot. At the front we won't even smell corporal's stripes."

The veterans growl and grouse, but they'd be the first to prevent a newly arrived sous-officier from making a blunder in action.

As night falls, all that is left of the regiment reforms, and starts off on a long dreary trudge across country—through shell holes filled with mud and water—quickly past French batteries in action, before the Germans reply—halting for a moment to let the tail catch up. Each stop and start spreads the column out, so now the men at the end are running in a feverish effort to keep up.

Six vicious cracks overhead! The Germans are sweeping the roads with Austrian 88's. and 130's. One or two shrieks, a little confusion; the stretcher men pass along the line to find the wounded, and the column moves on. There is little talking, and that in low tones, as if the men

* Old Soldiers way of speaking about newly made non-coms. Non-coms are animals till proved otherwise. "Sardines" slang for sergeants' chevrons.

## TEN THOUSAND SHALL FALL

are afraid of starting the shelling again—the same feeling one has on a mountain trail, where avalanches lie in wait for the loud-voiced traveller.

Soon we are at a huge dark mound, and word comes back that it is the redoubt of Vaux; we are to relieve the present garrison. Then begins a weary wait while they bring out their wounded. Pitiful sights—some of them, hobbling along between two friends, then an endless procession of stretchers—among them, the "basket cases." Why they don't put them out painlessly, then and there, is beyond civilized intelligence. Mere trunks, both arms and legs shot off, some of them blind as well, what possible use can they have for life, except that horrible instinct to live? Yet they must be carried for miles, go through torture in hospital, and drag out lives of helpless hell, to satisfy a squeamish sentimentality we called humanity.

> "Here are the needles. See that he dies
> While the effects of the drug endure. . . .
> What is the question he asks with his eyes?
> Yes, All-Highest, to God, be sure."

The last of the wounded disappear into the night, and we move into the redoubt, while the

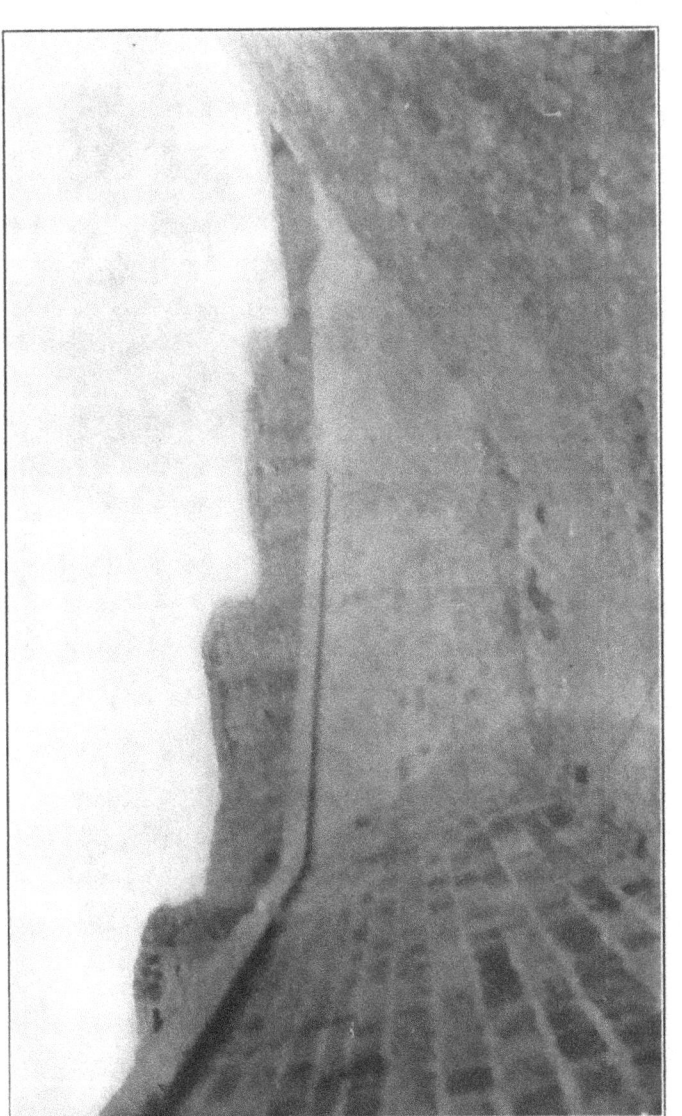

*The redoubt of Vaux, Verdun, March 1st, 1916.*

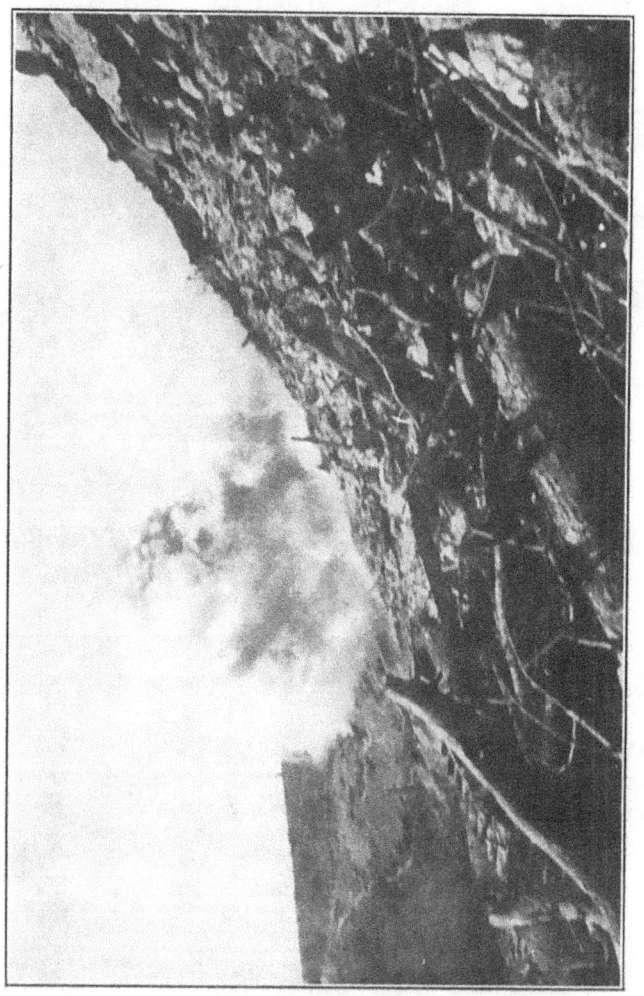

*Verdun, April, 1916.*

## VERDUN—SHOCK TROOPS

other battalion files down to the village to dig in and create a first line of defense . . . . Barricades are built of everything they can find. Houses are ransacked for mattresses to be used as sand bags. Then the clown in all soldiers comes out. Absurd figures dance around the streets dressed up in everything they can lay hands on, from top hats to petticoats. Men in the most fantastic mixtures of full dress uniforms of officers. One soldier dressed as a woman minces along putting up a ridiculous small parasol every time a shrapnel bursts. A wedding procession forms, but the shelling becomes serious, and everyone scuttles for cover.

The village of Vaux and the newly made trenches are raked from one end to the other. As house after house is crushed and crumpled into smoking ruins, the survivors take to the trenches.

All eyes are strained toward the edge of the slope leading up to the village, expecting each minute to see the grey-green wave of the attack surge over it. Then a sinister heart-stopping whistle. A blinding flash—an almost simultaneous series of crashes which dislocate the pit of the stomach, prolonged by the roar and rumble of falling tiles and masonry. The survivors turn to the wounded. Another salvo,—the solid, stone house is a gutted shell, one side strewn across the street. A sharp order to evacuate, and the men spring to pick up their helpless comrades. But a third salvo strikes, and all are buried under a smoking pile of beams and bricks. In the meantime the trenches are catching it. Retarded fuse shells and shrapnel, a sullen subterranean rumble and yards of the line are hurled into the air—men, sacks, rifles, *gabions* and earth, all falling back in a torn and tortured heap, while shrapnels crack like demon whips over all. The shelling redoubles,—then a nerve-shattering calm. The veterans know—their shrill cry of warning comes down the line.

"*Attention! Ils vont donner!*" As if conjured up by the cry, a solid green-grey mass of men rolls over the rise in front. Crash! The salvos once more before their barrage lifts from our front line. Firing breaks out in vicious crackling bursts, and the machine guns take it up with their steady wop, wop, wop, wop, wop. The firing increases spasmodically as the reserves from the redoubt arrive in the first line in breathless handfuls. But the mass of *veld-grau* rolls on.

## VERDUN—SHOCK TROOPS

Heavy toll is taken, but they are advancing in the famous mass formation, and as soon as one man drops another takes his place and the line seems impervious.

We are praying for our guns to put down a barrage, and cursing the gunners. A single rocket goes up from the fort. "What the hell's the use of lengthening the range; don't they know we want a barrage!" Ten seconds later, two white rockets go up and almost immediately the 75's come into action. To us it is the most cheering sound in the world, that continuous roll —like drums—the sharp, spiteful crack of the shells! The whole German line is blotted out in gobs of thick white smoke. Great gaps have been torn in the line. The attack wavers, stops, fails.

This lasts all day. Seven times the attack surges over the rise, seven times it breaks, and retires under the combined rifle, machine, and field gun fire.

The four companies in the redoubt are copping it, too. One company is in bomb-proofs under the main rampart, but these shelters are only protected in the rear by a *parrados* some twenty feet back. A three hundred and eighty millimetre

## TEN THOUSAND SHALL FALL

shell bursts in the open space and the shelters become a shambles. Of the two hundred and fifty men, only six survive, and the walls are plastered with blood, brains and bits of smoking uniform.

March 2, 1916.

"DEAR GERALD:

......  The shelling has become so fierce today that we can't keep anyone on deck, and are all huddled inside the so-called bomb proofs, which the boches are chewing big pieces out of at each shot. I feel a lot better now, but a few minutes ago the shock of the shell and the blasts made me faint and sick, and I had to lie flat till the blood ran back again. The boches are attacking now, and our *feu de barrage* of big guns and field pieces and their preparatory bombardments are something hellish. I hope you don't mind my writing you these things, but I want to register them with someone who can keep them. They should be interesting later. They have just shot away a whole corner of this redoubt—and the damn thing was made of reinforced concrete and steel plates. The devils have been at it for nearly four hours now with an average of one shot a minute at this particular little redoubt. I mean one big shell of 210 or 380 mm. caliber. The little ones only help to make a row and sweep the ramparts. Allah knows how long this old box will hold together. We laugh and munch army biscuits and

smoke, but there is cold death in the eye of every man. Some of the men are fast asleep—sheer nervous exhaustion. I took some pictures yesterday of this dump before the real riot started. If I can, I'll get some of what it looks like after it's over. Goodbye old man, more later if I can. Keep this.
Affec.,
Ding."

The inside of the casemate looked like Goya's picture of a madhouse. No room to lie down and no benches to sit on, we squatted on our heels. Here and there a smoky kerosene lamp lit up a group of faces, hollow-eyed, gaunt. We had to relight the lamps continually as the concussion of direct hits blew them out. Periodically, the silence in the room was broken by a shout from the man nearest the door. "Sentinel's killed! Send up another!" Then a slight commotion as the next man on the list groped his way to the door, and almost certain death.

Suddenly a cry from above galvanizes us into action. "They are coming!" The major telephones desperately to the brigade commander asking for a barrage. *"Hallo! La brigade! Faites donner les soixante-quinzes devant Vaux!"* No answer. The sergeant telephonist

## TEN THOUSAND SHALL FALL

almost tears off the handle in his effort to ring through—the wires have been cut. "Two runners."—They go.—"They are down, Captain."—"Two more." "One of them is through. No, he is down too." "Fire the two rockets." (The signal of the day for a barrage.) One of them misses fire—(Oh, Christ—is everything against us!) At last the signal is given; and as the 75's begin to roll, we pile out of the fort to reinforce the first line.

\* \* \* \* \* \*

March 3.
"Dear Gerald:
Well, we got out of that bombardment all right, but I hope I never have to go through the like again. They burned up 1,200 big shells on that little fort alone, all 15 or 10 inch. Good Lord, things are moving fast! Last night we were in reserve waiting to attack. We rushed six miles to get into position, and at the top of a hill were met with gas shells. We had to catch our breaths in our respirators. Like eating a banana under water, it can be done, but it's difficult. . . . . ."

At dawn we moved out of the woods and advanced toward Fleury. Word was passed around that we were to attack and take it, and then continue toward Douaumont. The usual

## VERDUN—SHOCK TROOPS

soldiers' grousing broke out on every side. "What! Attack after two days with nothing to eat! Just let them give the order, they'll see what'll happen. I'm going to throw up my hands and go kamarad" . . . . But when the whistle blew we went forward like fresh troops.

French soldiers are a cool lot. We were taking cover behind a railway embankment before the final rush to take the village. Everyone knew we were to attack within the next minute, but each was attending to his own little affairs as if he were in rest billets. I was having quite a struggle with a dead Algerian. My rifle was broken, and I had a shrewd suspicion I might need it in the house to house fighting ahead of us, so I tried to borrow one from the dead *"Bikho."*\* I grasped it firmly by the muzzle and pulled, but the *Bikho's* hands were locked around the trigger-guard and sling, and he clung to it in grim death. Then I tried a little pressure with my foot on his chest, but though his arms gave, he still hung on. So I borrowed one from a less tenacious stiff. Some of the men were writing post cards; they explained it was not often they had a chance to write just before an attack.

\*Slang for Algerian Soldier.

## TEN THOUSAND SHALL FALL

Others were busily hunting in the packs of dead men for emergency rations.

At the preparatory command we crouched ready to spring forward. *"En avant!"* And we flowed over the embankment, like water over a dam; greeted by a murderous fire from the German batteries. The station of Fleury was enveloped in a red haze as shell after shell hit the red-tiled roof. The village was like a gigantic Noah's Ark hammered to pieces by a child. The streets were littered with dead cows and horses, lying on their backs, all four legs stiff in the air. Furniture abandoned by the refugees was scattered everywhere, and chickens and ducks fled squawking before us. We took the village in a series of short rushes, but the Germans pulverized it with shell fire and as we advanced we lost heavily. Once Fleury was cleared, the regiment was reformed and we started off in the direction of Douaumont. The original intention was to take the village that night, but casualties were so heavy that it was decided to wait for what was left of the second battalion before pushing on. So we crouched in a valley where we were spotted by airplanes and shelled till nightfall.

## VERDUN—SHOCK TROOPS

At dusk I took a detail of sixteen men down to bring up food. This not being the Foreign Legion, the soup kitchens were considerably in the rear; in fact it took us four hours to find them. The comments of some of the old Légionaires were acid. The negro prize fighter was mumbling and grumbling to himself as he forged through the mud. "What's the matter now, Bob?" "Hungry yesterday. Hungry today. Hungry the day before. Don't care how soon my military experience terminates." Neither did I.

We had to keep to the roads, as the mud was impassable in the open fields; but on the other hand the roads were being continually swept by a fire from Austrian 88's and 130's, the shells that give no warning. Between Fleury and Souville the road was strewn with broken artillery wagons, exploded caissons, mangled and puffed-up bodies of horses, men, rifles, equipment, baby carriages, mattresses and bird cages.

Finally we discovered the field kitchens and fell to for a square meal before starting back—natural but imprudent. You can't go three days without food and then gorge: two minutes later we slid our lunches to a man, and compromised on a cup of coffee apiece. The stew might have been edible when we left, but it was nothing but cold grease by the time we reached the line.

Of the sixteen, who started out, seven got back. We arrived at the edge of the wood, just at dawn, and then the worst happened: in the final rush to the trenches, the man carrying the two canvas buckets of coffee was hit, and of course fell on them as he went down. This was bad, for the men in line had been two days with nothing to drink. Some of them scooped up snow and ate it, which only made matters worse, adding dysentery to thirst.

Dawn and fresh complications. The village of Douaumont was not held, as we had supposed, by French Infantry, but by German machine guns, and our line was exposed to fire from the right flank and rear. Sandbags had to be placed —at any price. . . .

The morning mist cleared, and we stared on our handiwork. Line after line of grey-green German dead lay stretched in front of us, piled three feet high in spots—almost as if the slow-rolling waves, that come after a storm, had been frozen as they climbed the beach.

## VERDUN—SHOCK TROOPS

Heads rose from the enemy's trenches. Germans and French stood up and looked at each other at a distance of only forty yards numbed. Nobody fired, nobody spoke. Both sides were fought to a standstill. . . .

At nightfall sounds of arriving reinforcements came from the German lines, and we prepared to repel a fresh attack. But there was stealthy movement behind us, and *"Chasseurs Alpins"* began dribbling into the trenches. Our relief had come also—and just in time. We had scarcely dropped over the hill into comparative safety when the German attack broke loose. But they were met by fresh troops, and we could hear the yells of the *"chasseurs"* driving forward a counter attack.

All we could think of was our thirst. I waded into a shell hole and drank greedily from the green-scummed water. A rocket flared up—what I had taken for a log, lying in the pool, was a corpse! I didn't give a damn, only glad I had drunk before I saw it. A shell burst unpleasantly close and I lumbered after the disappearing section.

## TEN THOUSAND SHALL FALL

From a letter:—

". . . . . . Next day, we hung around in some woods about three miles back of the line in reserve. As luck would have it, the Boches chose that day for a systematic search of the surrounding country with their big guns. They began at six in the morning and kept it up until five that night. I saw whole squads of men go up twenty feet in the air, sacks on their backs, and come down a shower of arms, legs, heads and red hash. That night, we pulled out for the rear, and marched fifteen kilometres. You may guess what condition we were in when I tell you two men dropped dead from exhaustion. We stayed a day in a little town, and then marched twelve kilometres, where we took autos, just back of Verdun. Another man dropped dead on the way. The autos took us to a village about 60 kilometres off. We stayed there one day, and then started marching 25 miles a day. The next three days were like a nightmare to me. I couldn't eat, and I had the colic and dysentery as had over 75% of the men. How we ever marched is a mystery; every day men dropped dead. Anyway, here we are for a few days rest. The brigade went into it with 5,500 rifles, and came out with 1,100, but we stopped em, by God.

Best luck, old man, and write soon.
Affec.,
Ding."

*Chapter Nine*

## VERDUN AGAIN—AND SPRING

WITH the fresh drafts Ole Neilson, a huge Swede who had been wounded in the Legion, joined the 170th. During his long stay in hospital he had got badly out of hand, and I had a job keeping the peace between him and Georges, our sergeant. I finally persuaded Georges that if he would be lenient with Neilson in rest billets, he would find him worth the trouble in line. In consequence Ole stuck to me like a big overgrown puppy. We shared everything, though I was not partial to the tins of dead fish and other Swedish delicacies he got from home.

25th April. Orders to move up. Verdun again. Bad news. Everyone gloomy. Motor trucks. They evidently need us badly.

26th April. *Faubourg Pavé*—not so bad. Found pianola—wild night.

27th April. Hear we're to go up into line tonight. Rumors say counter attack. Everyone pretty sober. The very names around here are ominous. *Mort Homme-Ravin de la Mort.* Even Vaux and Douaumont sound like big guns.

The long blue column trudged in silence through the town; shoulders hunched, jaws thrust forward—dogged resignation. On the outskirts of the *Faubourg Pavé* a mechanical piano in a ruined café came suddenly to life under the ministrations of some Zouaves, and jangled out *"Mariette."* Magic! Squad after squad took up the refrain and with roars of laughter waltzed up the road. A hundred yards further on the music died away, and gloom settled down once more.

Past Souville, down through Fleury (now nothing but a hole in the ground), swinging to the right of Douaumont we finally halted on the other side of the valley of the Bois de Chapîtres.

Then came the weary business of a relief. Ten steps forward. Stop. Ten minutes wait, punctuated by raking shell fire groans of the wounded and curses from the rest of us.

*"Bon dieu! Qu'ést ce qu ils foutrent la bàs?"* (Good God! What the hell are they doing over there?)

Finally however, by shuffling and pushing, it

## VERDUN—AND SPRING

was over. Ole and I found ourselves in a shallow dugout along the Décauville ledge. He had forgotten a lot of his trench warfare cunning, and his rage was comical on discovering that someone in the other regiment had exchanged a filthy, mud-crusted rifle for his own nice clean one which he had left outside the dugout.

All morning shells howled over the crest of the hill back of us and burst in the valley below. Ole was an optimist.

"By yiminy Dave, I tink we're in a dead angle. Dey can't reach us here!"

My gloomy reply, "There ain't no such animal in this God damn war," was drowned by a formidable explosion ten yards off. Three seconds later there was a dull thud just outside and going out to investigate we discovered a 210" shell, which fortunately had not exploded. A slow smile crept over Ole's face and he burst out laughing.

"By yiminy you bane right. Dere ain't no such animal!"

For two days preparations were made for a counter attack. All the work was done under heavy bombardment and losses were according. An old quarry was turned into an ammunition dump and filled with small arms, 37" hand grenades and trench mortar bombs, as reserve ammunition for the attack.

Next day a shell lit bang in the middle of it and the ammunition went skyward in one glorious explosion, taking twenty men with it.

We seemed to be dogged by bad luck. As we stood to, ready to go over, the company on our right was practically annihilated by four 155" shells from French batteries—shorts. Result—when we went over, our right flank was dangling in the air. We gained our objective and dug in, but were exposed to galling enfilading fire and were outflanked by a counter attack of grenadiers of the Prussian guard. They came forward running zig-zag, hurling potato-masher grenades. It was a wonderful occasion for sport from the point of view of shooting—either you got the man before he threw the grenade, or the grenade got you.

The support troops came up on the right flank and the serious business of consolidating the position began.

Ole was now in his stride. During a food fatigue once, the detail ran into a barrage. Six men were killed and one wounded. The others

## VERDUN—AND SPRING

waited in shell holes, hoping for it to lift. Not so Ole. Carefully depositing his soup kettles in a shell hole, he picked up the wounded man and carried him to Fort Souville. The detail was still waiting when he got back. Announcing that the men in line were hungry, he picked his buckets up again, and walked straight on through the barrage. In three days he won three citations.

Meanwhile my backbone got in the way of a bit of shrapnel and I was ordered down with the next convoy of wounded, for treatment and rest. At nightfall we started. Somebody strapped my pack on my shoulders for me, and I followed the walking cases. Down across the valley, stumbling into shell holes and tripping over the corpses that littered the narrow path, now in inky darkness, now in the blinding light of a rocket, we shoved along in fearful haste. The ground was swept, from time to time, by salvos of high explosive shells. Sometimes they took their toll, and the surgeons' work was reduced. The Fort of Souville rose in front of us and in we all crowded. We found ourselves in a jumble of troops, horses and wagons, and stretcher bearers, waiting for the storm of shells to abate before continuing on their divers missions.

I left the Fort and wandered back to the *"Maison Blanche,"* a clearing station, hoping for a ride on the running board of an ambulance to *Faubourg Pavé*. The house was dark, but from somewhere in the back came low moans. Groping my way along, I opened a door and stepped into a medieval torture chamber. On the floor writhed a huge black Moroccan, held down by four *infirmiers*. The sweat of agony was on him. His eyes rolled white— he groaned through his clenched teeth—bright red blood gushed over his black skin from a jagged wound in the groin. Two, white-coated surgeons worked with fiendish intensity. And flickering candles threw grotesque, reaching shadows on the ceiling. . . . The post had evidently run out of morphia. Thirty yards down the road I saw the house go up in splinters as a salvo of heavy shells struck home. All that pain and trouble for nothing!

\* \* \* \* \* \*

At the *Faubourg Pavé* the search for quarters was a nightmare. The place was infested with Algerian troops, none too friendly to a lone

## VERDUN—AND SPRING

French soldier at best; and by now my arms were hanging limp and paralyzed.

I couldn't light a candle; the only way to find a safe place for the night was to try the doors with my shoulder, and if they opened, to listen for breathing. At last I found an empty room, and went to sleep with my feet planted against the door, and my sack still strapped to my back. Next day I found the wagon train and a doctor, who patched me up in record time. . . .

In my absence Ole had been distinguishing himself further. During a German counter attack, he recovered one of our machine guns, turned it on them, and when the ammunition was exhausted, retired carrying it with him.

I was still on the sick list, but had volunteered to take a message up to our major, in line. At Souville I was told the regiment was being relieved, but that the major was still in the trenches. So off again, with two Red Cross men as guides. We had barely started when all Hell broke loose. The stretcher bearers, pointing to the left, shouted some garbled directions and disappeared into the night. For a moment I was completely lost, but the flash of the next salvo showed me the path lined with dead. I was guided across the valley by the flash of shells, and I knew, each time I stumbled over a corpse, that I was on the right road. Suddenly a rocket disclosed a little procession twenty yards to my right. Four stretcher bearers with their usual load, followed by a lanky figure I would have known anywhere.

"Ole!"

"Py yiminy! Is that you Dave? Dey tell me you're dead. See you later." Then, as an afterthought: "Py Christ, I'm glad you're not!"

We passed, on our lawful occasions. I heard the story later. During the relief, the remains of the third section had been practically wiped out by a barrage. Six men had been killed outright, the sergeant and another, wounded. The other man ran for the dressing station, but Georges was badly hit—eye, both wrists, and side.

At this point Ole stepped in. Sitting calmly beside him, he cut the sergeant's equipment to pieces, made tourniquets of the straps, and stopped the bleeding of one wound after another. Then he waited. Presently four stretcher bearers hurried along and he hailed them. Georges was too weak from loss of blood, to

## VERDUN—AND SPRING

walk, but on hearing he was not wounded in the legs, the stretcher bearers refused to carry him. Ole admitted having lost his temper. Georges told me afterwards, he was afraid Neilson was going to clean them up. Anyway, cocking his rifle, he convinced them it was healthier to carry the sergeant in—they were doing so when I passed them.

* * * * * *

Spring—and six whole weeks in front line trenches in a quiet sector. Wild flowers grew along the edge of the trenches, and some little brown birds were nesting in the eave of our dugout. Between bombardments, came the calls of thrushes and blackbirds and finches—once I heard a lark. There were drawbacks of course, other than rats and shells. The Germans had three mines under our lines; we could hear their sappers working at others, and wondered, vaguely, when they would be touched off. The muffled subterranean tapping day and night, might have got on our nerves, but how could we worry with the sun shining! Days of quiet reading, bathing in the canal, endless games of *"Manille,"* and symphonies on cigar box fiddles. Besides, the battle of the Somme was raging,

## TEN THOUSAND SHALL FALL

and we were wondering when our turn would come.

Before the end of July we pulled out of line, and moved up to the Somme sector.

*Chapter Ten*

## BATTLE OF THE SOMME

ALL around us was activity and hustle; parks of Artillery waiting to go up into line, shell dumps, barbed wire duck boards and all sorts of stores, ammunition, and equipment. Narrow gauge railways spread out in all directions, and every ten minutes a toy train loaded with enormous shells puffed busily on its way to the forward ammunition dumps.

The roar of guns was continuous night and day; and from dusk till dawn a flickering, red glare lit the horizon.

July 25th, 1916.

"DEAR GERALD:

. . . . . . We are moving up again shortly. At present we are in wooden huts about seventeen miles from the front. The band is giving a concert, and over the music you can hear a continual booming—the most devilish bombardment I have ever heard. It makes you feel as if you were at a comic opera, with a storm gathering, while the villagers stroll about the plaza. It would be funny if we had not been there before and

## TEN THOUSAND SHALL FALL

did not know what all the cannonading meant. I hope I get plugged this time for better or worse. I'm tired of being the lone, last survivor of gory battlefields, the only human, civilized eye witness, so to speak. God! how those guns are roaring! I have never heard anything like it before. Wish we would hurry up and get into it. Funny—I'll be nervous as a marmosette now till I get right into the first line, and they start bursting over us. Always the same—almost trembling till the riot starts, and then feeling like a kid going home for Christmas vacation. . . . . . .

July 28th.

. . . . . . The flag was decorated this morning, so we should be on our way ere long! I'm pleasantly confident that I'm going to be wounded this time—My God, it's about time—two years without a rest is enough for any man. . . . . . .

July 30th.

. . . . . . Here we are, eight miles nearer. We can smell the powder and corpses. One regiment of our Division attacked last night. The 174th attacks tonight, and we will probably attack tomorrow. . . . . . .

August 2nd.

. . . . . . Hell of a big explosion just now. Whole sky red. Shells popping like a curtain fire. . . . It's all hell to pay somewhere and no pennies hot. . . . . . .

August 3rd.

. . . . . . Know all about it. One of our shell and hand grenade depots went up in a blaze of glory, and

## THE SOMME

killed about twenty men. Lucky it wasn't the 15-inch shell depot. The second zouaves of our division have been relieved. Came down cut to pieces, one battalion cut up and captured; the other two with about 150 men apiece left. . . . . .

August 5th.
Seems we are to have the honor of attacking Clery. Whether we take it or not remains to be seen. It is the worse sector on the French front in these parts. This seems to be the devil's own fight, but it can't be one hell of a lot worse than Verdun. . . . . ."

On August eleventh the regiment moved up. As night fell we trudged along the road, a high hill on one side and a river and marshes on the other. Almost immediately we came under fire of the German long-range guns. Some of the shells plopped harmlessly into the river; others burst on the cliff above us, and some took their toll. Then we came out on the level, passing through the ruins of Veaux (Somme)—the ghastly skeleton of what had once been a village. Marching along its main street, we clambered out of one big shell hole full of water into another, finally reaching the third line and effected the relief, then out on a work party.

# TEN THOUSAND SHALL FALL

August 13th.

". . . . . . Just got back from working between the first and second lines in plain day. Of course, we were shelled out by high explosives. Damn that fool Captain of ours. . . . . . At present we are in reserve for two divisions. If anything goes wrong, we stop the gap. Hell of a job, for we will have to come up under heavy shell fire after the attack has started. There was a little fog this morning, so their fire on our trenches was poor, but now it is a beautiful day, and they are dropping them all around and into us.

11 A. M. Aug. 13 (?) By golly, they wanted to send us out again. But the lieutenant sent us back. My Lord, those guns are busy. They are beginning to strafe our part of the line now. They move up and down the line, concentrating, and giving each a bit of music for a while, and then move on. This war gets worse and more terrible every day, Gerald. I don't see how flesh and blood stands it. It makes me sick when some bloated profiteer sits in his armchair in Paris and talks about going on to the limit. If those people had to go through 16 hours shelling, and didn't die of heart failure, we would have peace tomorrow. And don't you believe all those hardy poilu yarns. They are spun by men in the reserve who spend all their time in quiet parts of the line, where they have shelters 40 feet deep and get about ten field gun shells a day. I think this war must be getting on my nerves,

## THE SOMME

for every day I get more and more fretful, and I used to like these affairs . . . .

. . . . The attack has started. The minute they saw our men on the parapet, a lot of Germans came running over, hands up, and cursing the Kaiser. They were knocking hell out of our trenches.

Aug. 14, 12:30 P. M. At five prompt, last evening, we started off. We had communication trenches for about 200 yards, and then they thinned out into mere ditches. Imagine lines of men, Indian file, rushing down the ditches, crouching in the deeper places to catch their breath, then rushing over the shallow ones, mouths coated with dust and powder fumes, and hearts as big as toy balloons from the running and excitement. Big shells dropping on each side of the trenches. We climbed out to cross a road and had a glance at what was going on. The first and second waves were 500 yards ahead, deployed in open order, and going like hell. But there was a machine gun tickling our flank, so we rushed across the road to take advantage of the bank on the other side. Then open country again, and catching it from everything.

The German machine gun nest on the left began to cripple the attack. This meant the regiments on our left and right would go forward, flanks in the air.

Our major sized it up at a glance, and decided to sacrifice his battalion. "Face to the left! Open order! Grenadiers forward! Go and get 'em!" It cost six hundred men, but the battalion coming on behind us went through clear. Finally we got into position. The 2nd and 3rd battalions had taken the trenches, and we were four hundred yards back of 'em in an open field as reserve. We were told to dig ourselves in as best we could. I went back to some boche rifle pits to get some big tools. You should have seen the work of our 75's. Every damn pit was full of dead bodies. Disgusting sight—still pink and white instead of the yellow and black they will be—flies all over them. I found my tools and started digging with Neilson, my fighting mate. Just as we got started he was called away to go on a water detail. At sundown, 8 o'clock, the boches started a counter attack, and started bombarding the landscape. Their big high explosives were bursting two or three yards from my hole, but I was so tired I went to sleep in spite of them. At midnight, someone landed all fours on my chest, and lay down beside me. I thought it was Neilson, but it was someone else. He lay there for a while, but they landed a couple of big ones near us, and he cleared out. I was just getting to sleep when someone else crawled in. He stayed a while, till they began to get unpleasantly close, and then persuaded me to make a break for some rifle pits to the left. When we got there, he disappeared, and I spent a miserable quarter of an hour trying to find a place. Just then they began shelling the pits, and men dropped so fast that I decided to go home. There I found a friend who, while I was visiting, had had a shell drop on him, fortunately a dud. We dug out the pit and went to sleep. About 4 A. M. another boche attack broke loose. Next night

*The second company continues to advance. (250 men+4 machine guns leaves 10 men.)*

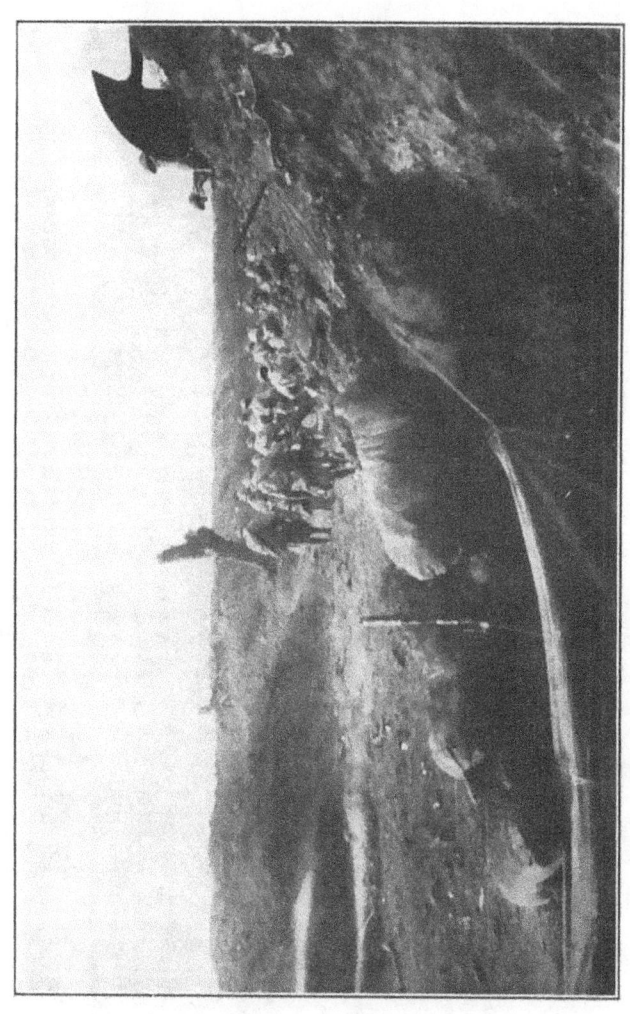

*Into the first German line, Somme, 1916.*

## THE SOMME

Neilson came back. He couldn't get back the night before on account of continual curtain firing. He had hardly arrived before I was called up for a food detail. Two miles there and back. It's bad enough scurrying over bad places, corpses, and marmite holes, with a rifle and equipment, but when you have a couple of soup kettles, as well, it's pure hell. . . .

6:30 P. M. There is something up on our left. The 75's are rolling like drums, and the boches are bombarding to keep them quiet and under cover. I think we were to attack, but the boches may have beat us to it. Their curtain fire is getting nearer and nearer our dugout. God help us now.

August 13th, 7:45 P. M.

Well, they seem to have let up for a bit. They may begin again any minute, and it only takes one shell to do the trick, but it's different from seeing those big shells creep nearer and nearer, exploding in perfect time. Hell, they are at it again. The worst of it is they don't let up at sundown—on the contrary; and shell fire is twice as terrifying at night. At least to me. . . . . . More later, perhaps.

Ding."

The shells descended upon us, and Ole and I crouched in our shelter, smoking furiously.

"Well Ole, it looks as if we're in for it this time. Do you believe there is anything on the other side?"

"I dunno. I don't believe much in nothing." And, with his usual afterthought: "Anyway, if a shell bane hit this dugout we bane go together."

We were interrupted by a series of crashes and screams from the pits some twenty yards back, and rushed over to see what we could do. One of the young class was standing with his back to the parapet, breathing spasmodically, a glassy look in his eye and the whole back of his head blown off. No time to waste on him—reflex action. (I once saw a man buried with the earth heaving up and down, from muscular convulsion, as they covered him.) The others were in a bad way. One was disemboweled, and the sergeant was screaming—and with cause. Both legs were shattered, but the thing that broke his nerve was a shrapnel bullet through the palm of his hand. We dug them out and bandaged them. The poor devil started screaming: "Put me out of it! Be good fellows, and put me out of it! I'm done!" We reassured him in one breath and cursed the Boche in the next: "You're all right old man. Steady on. The stretcher bearers will be along presently—God damn those Christ-bitten .... Hope to hell we get an-

## THE SOMME

other chance at them before we clear out!" I gave him one of my morphine tablets. That left one for Neilson and two for me; one for a wound, and two to go out with if I were badly crippled.

The morphia began to take effect, and the sergeant quieted for a moment. Suddenly he screamed again, and then, in a strange, small voice:

"Can't you stop that man screaming? He's getting on my nerves."

The stretcher bearers turned up. I scribbled a label that he had had morphine, and stuck it in his tunic. Twenty yards to the rear all five of them were wiped out by a shell.

I had copped it in the groin the first day of the attack, but as Ole was firmly convinced that nothing would happen to him while he was with me, I tried to stick it out. After four days though, the pain was unbearable.

"Sorry Ole. Can't stick it any more. Try and get a light one yourself, and get to the same hospital."

"That's right. You got to go old man. Goodbye. I think I'll get it next time."

I dragged myself along to the clearing station,

where I was examined and ticketed. I took such of my things as the Red Cross men had not stolen, and crawled into an ambulance. I never saw Ole again. . . .

\* \* \* \* \* \*

The ambulance jounced over the rough roads.

"Stop! Stop! Oh, for God's sake stop. My shoulder. My poor leg!"

The driver was green and pulled up to see what was wrong. As he appeared at the door, he was greeted by a storm of protest.

*"Bougre de charroigne d' embusqué!* Do you want us to be killed, after getting this far back?—Get on—step on it—beat it!"

They dumped me in a hut on the outskirts of a field hospital, and there I lay, forgotten, in the rush to entrain the wounded. . . . Two days later orders came to evacuate the place, and in collecting the cots, I was discovered—so low, they rushed me to hospital at Amiens. The battle of the Somme was still going full blast, and the town was crammed with wounded and British staff. Every hospital was full—they finally found me a bed in the citadel. . . .

This place was a catch-all for the general overflow—everything from prisoners awaiting

## THE SOMME

court martial, to shell shock cases. One poor devil was muzzled and strapped to the bed, for he bit and clawed furiously at anyone coming within reach. Another was fully convinced that the whole damn war was being waged for the benefit of the moving picture companies. He refused to take his medicine, go to the shower bath or even get up, before he had been reassured that the lights were correct, and camera-men waiting and ready. A third had been blown up in a sapping operation. He was a public nuisance. At any hour of the night or day he would steal through the wards, open a *table de nuit,* tie a string to the vessel inside, and close the door again. Then came a regular ritual. Holding the string tightly in one hand, and striking an attitude, he would begin: *"Attention! Attention! Couchez-vous par terre, tous le monde. Tirez!"* [Everyone lie down! Fire!] On the last command the string was yanked, the little door flew open, and, crash. . . . !!! Satisfied that he had carried out his orders and blown up the bridge, or whatever it was, he would go back to bed and sleep for a few hours more. After the first two or three times, the sight of him creeping through the ward was enough to

## TEN THOUSAND SHALL FALL

set up a howl of rage from the rest of us. *"Bon dieu, c'est le fou, encore! Gardes les pots!"* (Good Lord, it's that idot, again! Look out!)

Military hospitals are wonderful things—in novels. Spotless, sun-lit wards, sympathetic doctors, charming Red Cross nurses, and well-behaved wounded. Propped up on fresh pillows, with neat strawberry stained bandages round their heads, they smile in heroic endurance. Emergency hospitals don't come up to scratch. The floors may be scrubbed, the walls and ceilings remain in status quo. Spiders have fled from the reek of disinfectants, but their deserted homes still wave gently in the breeze. Doctors are overworked—efficient but hectic; and the charming nurse is replaced by some fat old orderly, who, as a great favor, smuggles in wine—at a price. If rude and unromantic the treatment is effective, and wonderful operations have been done in these improvised hospitals.

*Chapter Eleven*

## I CHANGE ARMS—THEN ARMIES

"UNFIT for the Infantry. Send him to the Artillery."

The judgment of three medical colonels, after the doctor had drawn diagrams on me in blue pencil, and the oculist had put in his report. And so to the Artillery School at Satory. . . .

Satory was ten minutes from Versailles and only an hour from Paris. The major's striker sold bits of paper, stamped with the battery's seal, for a franc apiece. Then you wrote your own leave, made a squiggle for the signature, payed somebody three francs to replace you on guard duty—*et voilà!* Perfect—unless you were caught. Better still, Satory was only three miles from Buc, where I found many old friends who had transferred to the Aviation. One of them, a schoolmate, was *brigadier moniteur\** in

---

\*Corporals and sergeants in cavalry and artillery are called *brigadiers* and *maréchaux de logis.*

charge of the American *éléves pilots* (cadet pilots).

Pete was having a deuce of a time keeping the new ones in order. It was a different story from running a squad in the cavalry, with the discipline of the whole French Army to back him. They were nice boys and keen on the job. But they seemed to think that, having volunteered before America came into the war, they were released from all rules, regulations, and discipline to which the rest of the French Army might be subject. Quite a problem!

He thought of me. Foreign Legion from the beginning of the war—if I didn't know what discipline was, who did? The very motto, on the colors of the Legion, substitutes *"discipline"* for *"patrie."*—Just the man!

I was asked over to dinner, and the new recruits were invited to meet and talk with this veteran of two-and-a-half years. I gave a marvelous harangue on duty, discipline, and obligations. I got more smug with each drink. I pointed out that it was a fine act on their part to volunteer, that they deserved a great deal of credit for it, and that I was sure they would do well when they got to the front. At the same

## I CHANGE ARMIES

time, the fact that they had come of their own free will was offset by the point that they had been admitted, at once, into the most sought after arm of the service. That their French colleagues now training with them had only gained entrance to the school at Buc through conspicuous bravery, or wounds that incapacitated them for the Infantry or Artillery. Therefore, they all started on an equal footing, and they should consider themselves just as subject to regulations as the French!

I piled it on till Taps sounded, and started back to Satory. It was a dark night, and after two or three attempts to find my way through the woods, I gave it up and went back to the aviation school, returning to Satory for roll call next morning.

I slid into line just in time to answer my name, but I was told that the Captain wished to speak to me, at once. The interview was short but sharp.

"Where were you last night?"

"At the aviation school, Captain."

"What were you doing there?"

"Oh, just talking to some friends."

## TEN THOUSAND SHALL FALL

"Why didn't you return to the barracks in time for call over?"

"I lost my way in the woods."

"Hm! Bad as that, was it? Well, there was a counter roll call last night, and you were missing. I don't care whether you're an American or not—you must be taught that there is such a thing as discipline in the Army. You have come from the Legion; somebody should have hammered it into you by this time. No explanations! Shut up! Four days' prison."

So, for four days, the disciple of discipline meditated on the beauty of discipline—for others.

\* \* \* \* \* \*

We were trained on the old 155 guns—*Système Benge* breech—obsolete. Almost as dangerous to the gun crew as to the enemy! On the firing grounds . . . . a recruit pulled the lanyard—no result. Missfire! He opened the breech to see what had happened—the powder sack was smouldering. In a frenzy he tried to close and lock it, fumbling badly. With a backhander, the sergeant knocked him flying, and in the same stride threw open the breech. He yanked out the burning sack, throwing it on the ground, to burn harmlessly.

## I CHANGE ARMIES

"Gerbaut, four days' prison! That'll teach you not to monkey with a breech till five minutes after a missfire! If that powder had caught in the gun you'd all have been blown to bits. *Brigadier,* go on with the practice—" and he walked off to the infirmary, to have his burned hand dressed.

* * * * * *

Change of regiments. Due to mathematics at college, I was sent to a sound-ranging section at Vincennes. For a fortnight we did odd jobs around the Artillery barracks of the 13th field guns, waiting for our officers and apparatus to materialize. Here I got the reputation of a magnificent horseman. Though fairly well broken and trained, the Canadian remounts did not understand French, so the French drivers were up against it. "R-r-r-r-r!" they would say, the mustangs looked interested but unconvinced. *"Salles bêtes!"* They were as stubborn as mules. "B-r-r-r-r-r-r"—this time accompanied by a threatening gesture. The Canadians understood the gesture and registered indignation and restiveness. *"Qu'ils sont féroces!"* Stepping up to a horse, I grabbed the bridle: "Back up, boy— back!" A look of relief came over the mustang's face and he backed gently and gracefully, delighted to oblige. From then on I did overtime handling remounts.

We found a new way to get out of barracks. Forming in line, we would march across the yard, with an obliging corporal shouting fierce orders. "One, two—one, two! Left—Left—Left! Even if this *is* a fatigue, you're going to march in step!"

"Halt! Where are you going?" This from the sergeant on guard, at the gate.

"Fatigue to get hay." And we swung smartly out of the barracks, dispersing two hundred yards down the street, for the four corners of Paris.

It started at the "Hole in the Wall." Billy Dugan, some XVIth Canadian Highlanders and myself. We adjourned to Weber's—more drinks, and decided to hold Grand Fleet manoeuvers on the Champs Elysées. Seven *fiacres* were commandeered. The flag-ship was stocked with ammunition, rum, whisky and H. E. Brandy. Being in blue, I was Admiral. I named my Captains, and off we went: line ahead formation.

Every light, rakish craft on the horizon wanted to come alongside and board us; but, somehow,

## I CHANGE ARMIES

when women join a show of that sort, men disappear mysteriously. I signalled "repel boarders." This was neatly done by exploding our gas balloons with cigarettes.

The next evolution, line abreast across the whole avenue, brought down an attacking flotilla of police and *gendarmes*. They caught sight of me in French uniform, and the fight was on. Dugan was in blue too, but having eaten a tube of tooth paste he was foaming at the mouth. Not even the *gendarmes* cared to tackle that apparition. A brawny Highlander saved the day. Kilts flying, heedless of traffic, he tore down the line, bellowing:

"Change carriages! Race around the fleet and back!"

Instantly every one piled out, giving an imitation of a subway rush going to Jerusalem. The police fell back and we steamed full speed ahead for a restaurant in the Bois and scuttled our ships. . . .

. . . . The brawny Scot had been sinking lower, and lower. Of a sudden his eyes became fixed—he sat bolt upright—he bounded from his chair. Out on the road stood two steam rollers, deserted for the night. Inviting wisps of smoke floated from their chimneys. No need to explain—with a whoop they surged after him, and climbed aboard. The French have a huge sense of humor, but most *gendarmes* are Corsican—and I was A. W. O. L. anyway. When I last saw them, they were waddling down the road like outraged hens—the Great Steam Roller Race had started. . . .

\* \* \* \* \* \*

It was at Vincennes that Mata Hari was shot. Every week we were called out for military executions.

*"Mort, avec dégradation militaire."* For desertion in the face of the enemy, or in time of war—Death, with military dishonor. We used to laugh—what difference could it make, if they were going to shoot you anyway? That was in the early days. After we had seen our first execution. . . .

It might have been a parade, or an investiture. Everyone spick and span. The regiment in a hollow square—officers, colors, and band, in the centre. "To the Colors" the band blared out. *Was* this going to be an execution? Must be. There was the prisoner standing between a guard with fixed bayonets. "Right shoulder

## I CHANGE ARMIES

arms!" Yes, we usually presented arms at this point. Drums and bugles sounded "Attention!"

"Soldier Jean Dubois, class of 1898—married, father of three children. Croix de Guerre, two palms . . . . . desertion while on leave, and attempted escape to Spain. . . . . ." The voice droned on, "absent twenty days. . . . . . time of war. . . . . . tried by court martial. . . . . Dijon. . . . . . found guilty. *Mort avec dégradation militaire.*"

A group of non-coms gathered round the prisoner. When they stepped aside, his coat hung open and ragged—buttons, decorations, insignia were gone. We saw him start at one side of the square, the guard around him, hands clinched, head up, looking as if he'd see us all in hell. I think most of us were sorry for him . . . but he couldn't understand that, and only felt hundreds of eyes denying him. About half way, it began to get him. His head drooped—his hands hung loose. They took him around the whole of that dreadful square. . . . At the end, he could hardly shuffle along. I think he was in a sort of stupor when they put him up against the post, for he never made a sign when they asked him if he wanted his eyes bandaged. Then a squad, from another regiment, stepped up. And they shot him. . . . A little, crumpled heap on the ground. *"Mort avec dégradation militaire."*

\* \* \* \* \* \*

The life at Vincennes was too good to last. Our Lieutenant turned up while we were all A. W. O. L. in Paris, and decided that we had run wild quite long enough. Within a week we were on our way to the front.

There were thirty-five of us in the unit— mixed pickles. Barring those chosen for their mathematics, and kids who had volunteered before their class was called, we were all cripples.

Castagnole was a dark sallow boy, with a saturnine sense of humor. He had stopped a 77 with his back and was pronounced unfit for further service. After working in the Chemical Warfare Laboratory for three months, he volunteered for the front again. Though thoroughly disillusioned, and often in pain, he never shirked his job.

Red headed, hot tempered, Durupt had been a professor at the University of Nancy, but though he examined young officers in Mathematics, was only a corporal himself.

# I CHANGE ARMIES

The sergeant was an antique dealer, and our other corporal's chief claim to fame was the fact that he had sung with Mayol. I imagine it was a case of "Heinie played with Sousa once—but only once."

* * * * * *

At Boncourt in the St. Mihiel sector, no one wanted us. They seemed to think a Sound Ranging section would draw fire, so for weeks we were shunted from one farm house to another.

For awhile we found shelter in a *barraque Adrian*. It was bitterly cold. We had a miserable little stove, but no coal; even the partitions in the hut were coated with ice. The potatoes froze and in the Army when the potatoes freeze there is one result—scurvy. Our gums swelled and oozed black blood, but it wasn't till our teeth began to wobble that we recognized the trouble, and sent for lime juice and tinned vegetables. The hut was infested with cooties and fleas, but the last straw was added when one man spread the itch.

In spite of these little trials, we began the work of installing the section: building dugouts for the advance posts, setting up the microphones, cutting and planting telephone poles. This was

## TEN THOUSAND SHALL FALL

great fun as the ground was frozen hard, and a pick was as likely as not to bounce back and crack you over the shins. Then miles of telephone wire was strung out, connecting the posts with the central office; and finally the central itself was ready.

I soon discovered that life in the instrument room lacked privacy and independence, so when the wind and observation station was established, I put in for it.

The idea was to note the velocity and direction of the wind and temperature of the air every time a German shot was fired. When it came to running an *annomètre*, stop watch, telephone, twirl a thermometer on a string, and register everything in a note book, all in the same moment, I used to regret the loss of our caudal appendices.

I lived at the post, on a hill just over a wireless dugout. Somewhat exposed to wind and shell fire, but off duty I was master of my fate.

Boom! A shell would whirl overhead. Br-r-r-r-r would go the party wire, joining the outposts to central. The Lieutenant's voice "Hello! Posts one, two, three, four, five, six? Set your microphones." Ring—Br-r-r-r "Hello,

## I CHANGE ARMIES

the wind! They are firing." (You don't say so!)

I would climb out, set up my instruments, put on the telephone receiver, and hang the mouthpiece around my neck.

Boom!

"Shot P 1."

"Shot P 3."

"Shot P 4."

"Yes, Yes—Yes! Hello, P 2, didn't you hear it?"

"No."

"Hello, the wind! What's the direction?"

"40°—speed 60—temperature 10° C."

And so on this way for hours, rain or shine, till the German firing stopped.

Thunderstorms were not so amusing. The lightning would strike the wire and box my ears.

"Hello, Central! there's a thunderstorm overhead."

"Yes—yes! We know."

That was all the satisfaction I got.

I shared the dugout with a wireless operator, Oursan. He was twice my age—a master carpenter—hard boiled on the surface, but one of the whitest men I have ever known. We lived,

## TEN THOUSAND SHALL FALL

cooped up together in a tiny room for months, without a quarrel.

Post number three telephoned in one day, that Fritz was putting down a gas barrage and his gas mask leaked. The sergeant, knowing I was headed that way, asked me to take him up a new mask. I passed our dugout on the way. Oursan was watching the barrage between us and post number three.

"Hello, where are you going?"

"Nosal's gas mask is out of commission. I'm taking him up another."

"Through *that*?"

"Yes, I hope so."

"If that good for nothing, slack-jawed fool can't take care of his gas mask, why in hell doesn't he come down and get another, himself? What business is it of yours anyway? You're nothing but a god-damned half wit, forging through barrages for a fool like that. Here— you stay here—I'll take it."

"Nope, can't do it. Lessure told me to go."

"Told you—told you hell! Don't you know he couldn't *order* you to? It's a volunteer job. Oh, well, go ahead! But I wash my hands of you."

## I CHANGE ARMIES

So I went ahead, but Oursan went with me to the edge of the barrage.

Half an hour later I found him where I had left him—still cursing. He got distinctly rude when I asked him why he was waiting. But I saw he had his gas mask ready, and I knew my man. If I had been hit, I wouldn't have lain there long.

\* \* \* \* \* \*

I wore sabots stuffed with straw to keep my feet warm, and thought myself rather clever. Then I tried to climb down the ice-coated ladder. . . . I landed sudden and hard, and through some strange contortion, probably the same by which men acquire black eyes, stamped on my little finger. My hand got black—two days later I saw the doctor.

"*Tiens, tiens!* How did this happen?"

"I stepped on it."

"Are you trying to be impertinent?"

I explained the circumstances; he grunted, and took up a pair of scissors.

"Look the other way." . . . . I didn't try sabots again.

\* \* \* \* \* \*

"So you come from America?"

## TEN THOUSAND SHALL FALL

"Yes."

"Did you ever meet my cousin Jean Dupont? He went out to Buenos Ayres."

"No." And the conversation would languish.

When we declared war everything changed, and I was bombarded with questions. About this time I began to think I had better get into my own Army. My first application was returned with a note attached: If I would return to America and put in for Plattsburg they would consider my application. "Very much obliged to Jesus," as the British Tommies sang.

Through friends at court, I was allowed to take the exams in Paris, while on leave. The day came, and I presented myself—scared stiff. The three officers, who were to examine me, whispered among themselves; the Major (afterwards General) Nolan spoke.

"Mr. King, we don't know much about the French Army, and you probably know less about the American, so we don't see how we can examine you." My heart sank.

"But we have looked at your record and are proposing you for a first Lieutenancy, Infantry."

As I left the building, an officer was coming

*Where did that one go?*

*Going over the top, Somme, August, 1916.*

## I CHANGE ARMIES

up the steps. In my ignorance I mistook the black braid on his sleeve for a misplaced mourning band. There was something in his face, however, which spelt general, so I clicked to and saluted. Just in time! He seized an unobservant lieutenant by the arm and spun him round.

"You're in uniform! Are you a soldier, or not? If so, why the d—— can't you salute?"

He stumped upstairs, before you could say Black Jack—and General Black Jack himself it was!

\* \* \* \* \* \*

Back with the section—and life dragged along as it can, when you are waiting for an important letter. It was hot on the observation platform and I installed a barrel filled with water. Therein, I spent my time when not actually on the job. The Major passed one day just as I stepped out, and ran to tell Lieut. Delva that I had gone stark naked mad. Castagnole told me later, that when Delva explained I was American, a relieved smile came over the Major's face.

"Ah, I see! A redskin!"

From that time on, they spoke to me in the terms of Fenimore Cooper, "Oh, my Red

Brother," "Noble Watcher of the Winds," "Rain in the Face!"

Our Lieutenant worked us hard, but he didn't spare himself. We were a damned happy section, and I never saw an outfit where rank counted less.

The long expected official envelope finally arrived. Alas, it contained only an unsigned copy of an extract from a cable. True, it said I had been commissioned a 1st Lieut., Infantry, but Delva and others were not convinced. Letters to the Adjutant General's department were of no avail. I appealed to friends once more, and a signed and sealed notice arrived.

More complications! The American Army asked for my full record, with all changes of regiments, since enlistment. Delva wrote to the 5th Artillery, at Avranches, who referred him to the 13th F. A., at Vincennes. The 13th F. A. referred him to the 82nd H. A. at Satory. The 82nd H. A. referred him to the 170th Infantry, who referred him back to the 82nd H. A. Thereupon, the 82nd denied all knowledge of my existence, and considered the matter closed. Where *was* my record since I left the 170th? A day in Paris would have settled it all, but there was no

## I CHANGE ARMIES

chance of leave for months. However, regulations state that if a man is court martialed, and acquitted, he is entitled to 10 days leave. I asked to see the Major.

"*Mon Commandant,* I demand a court martial."

"On what grounds?"

"Desertion; from the time I left the 170th Infantry till I was transferred to this regiment."

"But this is serious!"

"It is, Sir. I'm in earnest."

"Voyons, Voyons, what's the trouble?"

Now a Major commanding the Artillery of a sector, has troubles of his own. He can't be expected to dry nurse every gunner, unless the gunner makes it plain that the safety pin is sticking into him. The moment I explained, he became human, and started buzzing off dynamic wires . . . .

Midnight—Oursan and I woke with a jump. Hammering on the door—and a liaison runner calling.

"King—King—your papers have come! You're to report at Central tomorrow, with all your junk, and you leave tomorrow night for the depot. Here—take your orders." He handed me an envelope, then stiffening up, he saluted. *"Bonsoir, mon lieutenant,"* and he left.

I turned, to find Oursan with tears streaming down his face, swearing like a trooper.

"It had to happen. I knew you would go, but it's damned hard. Just when I find someone I can get along with, off he goes! Still it's better this way—you'd probably be bumped off if you stayed. You always were a fool!" He grinned.

"We must celebrate! We'll eat up everything we have in the locker," and he set to work making coffee. . . .

The section had planned a send-off party for me, but it had to be shifted to midday, as the officers' mess had asked me to dine with them that night. As the party got under way, I began to have grave doubts if I would ever make dinner. Lieut. Delva saved the day by calling me into the office to clear up my papers.

"King, pardon, *mon Lieutenant!*"—he was only a 2nd Lieut.—"I'm taking the liberty of erasing the eight days prison I gave you."

"But why, Lieutenant Delva?"

"Well, I think you should leave this section with a clean slate. Besides, it strikes me as

## I CHANGE ARMIES

humorous for a sous-lieutenant to wipe out the crimes of his superior officer!"

"*Bien, Saint Pierre!*" I bowed, and emerged with a record white as snow.

Funny to be in an officers' mess after four years in the ranks. I felt shy at first, but I soon got over it, they were so damn friendly. . . A final toast—and Delva, the doctor, who was going on leave, and I started for the train.

Commercy—the station—the doctor and I leaned out of the window, waving as the train started.

"*Vive l'Amérique!*"
"*Vive la France!*"
"*Adieu—bonne chance!*"
"*A bàs les Boches! Adieu! Adieu!*"

Presently the conductor came along. He took one look at my ragged uniform, and scolded.

"Come on, get out of here! You go back to the third class. You have no business on an express, any way."

I tried to show him my papers, but he wouldn't look. The doctor came to my rescue.

"One moment, conductor. Try to be polite! Can't you recognize an American officer when you see one?"

## TEN THOUSAND SHALL FALL

The *controlleur* gasped, took one hurried look at my orders, and fled. The other officers in the compartment had been mildly curious on seeing a non-com in the first class, but had said nothing. Now, they suddenly came to life, insisted on our dining with them, and we all trooped to the dining car for a drink—to "wet my new stripes."

* * * * * *

If you suddenly jump from two woolen stripes to a silver bar, it is hard to realize that one first lieutenant more or less doesn't matter much in a growing army.

I reported for orders—then I reported again. Still nothing happened; so I wangled a passport, and went to England for Christmas. That did it! Just before I left the French army I had stepped too near an HE shell and a small sliver stuck in my lip. I pulled it out and thought no more about it. But Christmas dinner must have stirred things up, for within two days my good eye was closed by the swelling. Nothing for it but see a specialist, who popped me into a nursing home—acute blood poisoning.

The operation was a joke, at least for me. The surgeon didn't find it so amusing—as I was

## I CHANGE ARMIES

going under, I got the idea my gas mask was leaking, and started a free for all fight.

Two days with a wet compress over my face—I could neither see nor smoke. Pleasant, as a premature burial! Then I badgered a nurse till she cut a hole for my mouth, and lighted me a cigarette. The compress dried, and caught fire, and we both got hell from the matron.

Life was pleasant—good food, friends coming to see the little tin hero, and impromptu dances in the cellar, during air raids.

A telegram from a friend at G. H. Q. spoiled everything.

"No authority order you on duty from England. Return France or commission will be cancelled."

Yes, Yes, immediately—but how? My passport was a one way emergency affair, and I had counted on orders to get me back. Then I thought of two friends who were running the ordnance in France on a big business basis, in spite of a few generals and colonels. A telegram, and its reply—the ordnance in London obligingly faked me some orders, and back I went.

## Chapter Twelve

### .... AND PEACE?

". . . . . . will proceed to the casual officers depot at Blois and report to the Colonel commanding. The travel, etc. . . . . . ."

OH, help! Just what was a casual officers' depot? I soon found it was anything but casual.

The billeting officer handed back my orders.

"All right—report to the O. C. at the Barracks tonight, and to Colonel Pulen tomorrow."

"But I've got a room at the hotel."

"Well, you can stay there tonight, but tomorrow you shift. All officers under the rank of Major must live in barracks. By the way, you must be in quarters by nine p. m. sharp."

Then and there I realized I would have to get me an independent command. This place was about as casual as a penitentiary.

Next morning I saw Colonel Pulen. He was an old school artillery officer, with a sense of humor. Ten minutes' talk, and he appointed me

## AND PEACE

chief liaison officer, with an order for billets in town, and a pass to go anywhere any time.

My billets were opposite the *château,* and fairly comfortable.

Later, the old man from next door, hearing I had been in the French Army, called in state.

"Lieutenant, I come on behalf of my wife and myself, to ask you to stay at our house."

"But, Monsieur, I am extremely comfortable, and satisfied here."

"But, Lieutenant, you don't understand. We wish you to come as our guest. I have lost three sons in this war, and I should feel unworthy of them if I did not ask an American, who has served in our army, to use their rooms."

I went.

My first job as liaison officer was to accompany the Colonel and his adjutant on their first official call. The French *Commandant de Place,* a kindly white haired man, received us with a beaming smile. The Colonel started to speak in French.

*"Commandant, je vous présent mon ajudant."*

The old gentleman looked blank, and I could guess what was going through his mind. *Tiens, Tiens!!* These Americans are democratic—but is it necessary for a colonel to introduce his sergeant major?

I cut in with a hasty *"Capitaine adjoint, mon commandant,"* and his face broke into smiles, once more. Turning to me, he began the inevitable set speech:

"Kindly tell your Colonel that I am not only charmed and touched to be able to welcome the American Army here, but I am also delighted to make the acquaintance of such a distinguished officer. I cannot say how much it thrills me to see the streets of this old town thronged with the khaki clad progeny of the men who fought beside the legions of Lafayette and Rochambeau." etc., ad lib. . . .

It was worthy of the opening of a Y house on the fourth of July. I started to translate, but the chief cut me short.

"Stop! Shoot it back to him, and ask him when I can get those motor trucks."

I shot it back strong, finishing up with an impassioned appeal for the trucks.

The commandant answered, briefly but to the point.

"What's he say?"

## AND PEACE

"He says he hasn't got any trucks, but will get some for us."

"Then what the hell was all that spiel you gave?"

"Lafayette, and a few trucks."

The Colonel grinned; we made our bows, and left. Outside he turned to me.

"Will he really get 'em?"

"Yes, sir, if I keep after him."

"All right, now listen. I see we can't handle these people as we would at home. I'll tell you what I want, and leave the rest to you. My motto is, when you've tried everything, and can't make it work, why, go ahead, and do it anyway!"

\* \* \* \* \* \*

If I had had any sense I would have stuck close to that Colonel. As it was, I still took the war seriously, and got transferred to Chaumont.

Here I found myself in the G 2 B, or counter espionnage section. There was nothing to do but censor field clerks' fiction, and explain to visiting firemen, and generals, how a system of purely mythical control cordons worked.

This would not do. I was wearing out my best cord breeches on a hard wood chair, so I appealed to the sound ranging section. I talked with the officer in charge, who had told me to report to him as soon as I was commissioned. He had become a general, however, so I found myself appointed to the Statistical Department, Prisoners of War Section. You don't understand? Neither did I. There was hidden dynamite in that job. The first time an irate general rang up, and I had to say "Service of Statistics, statistical officer in charge," I knew they would break me for mocking the mighty. Besides, there were too many stars, and eagles, not to mention oak leaves, around Chaumont for a first lieutenant's comfort. Discipline was so highly developed, we used to salute any limousine, on sight, empty or not.

The wildest night club in town was a *patiserrie* with a sign "Exotic Delicacies." I never found out what they were, unless it referred to the two girls who ran it. Here, again, a mere first lieutenant started at a disadvantage. I decided to try for another independent command.

One of my best friends was at our Berne legation, and, unknown to me, was pulling strings to get me up there. One day, the Major called me in.

## AND PEACE

"Do you know Mr. Ellis Dresel?"

"No, sir."

"Do you know Mr. Dolbeare?"*

"In a way, sir." I was beginning to know my oak leaves, and meant to play safe.

"Well, they want you to go to Berne, and start an office for checking our prisoners of war."

"I think I could be more useful here, sir."

"Oh, you do, do you! Well, just let me tell you, you will go where we see fit to send you. The trouble with all you young reserve officers is, you don't seem to realize there's a war on . . . ."

"Yes, sir! No, sir!" and I went on my way rejoicing—once the door was closed.

Paris—civilian clothes—a diplomatic passport—and Excelsior!

\* \* \* \* \* \*

Berne was a maelstrom of intrigue and comedy. Most of the diplomatic corps lived at the Bellevue Palace. Allies on one side of the dining room—enemies on the other. Mutual glaring, and hate fests before meals. In the lounge every other chair was occupied by a wide spread newspaper, from which stuck out mys-

---

*Frederic Dolbeare, 2nd, Secretary, American Legation at Berne.

terious legs. If conversation turned to interesting topics, a pair of ears would protrude beyond the paper, betraying the presence of the enemy.

Our chief was a fire-eater, and longed to get to the front. He was a regular officer, and the amateur soldiers about him almost drove him wild. We meant well, but were more interested in results than in regulations.

"Lieut. X., you will proceed as per previous orders, and report to Countess (?) Stejjenska for information."

"Colonel, that woman hasn't a bit of real dope. And, I'm not sure she isn't double crossing us."

"You heard what I said . . . ."

"But, Colonel, it will gum the game!"

"Lieutenant, I've got *just* enough officers here to hold a court martial!"

"Sir, I would welcome a court martial!"

Interference, and business of calming both of them. . . .

When I got to Berne there were three separate fights going on. The French and English were at daggers drawn. Our assistant military attaché did not like the English, and wanted to play with the French. The French were afraid we would put our foot in it; and the English

## AND PEACE

were for using us, but mistrusted our intimacy with the French. Over and above all there was a row in our own camp, between the Military and the Red Cross. Squabbles and petty jealousy seemed to be in direct ratio to the distance from the front. I was, instantly, ordered to take over all arrangements for feeding our prisoners in Germany, but the Red Cross was handling it far better than we could ever hope to, with our limited means, and staff. The head was an international character, and his second is now Secretary of Labor. I had just enough sense to stick to the prisoner enquiry business.

This was only a half time job, and the Colonel jumped at the idea of my doing *contre espionnage* work. I broke in a sergeant major to do the desk work in the prisoner game, got a rubber stamp of my initials in case of my absence, and I was off on the trail of the wily spy. But to keep my independence, I made it plain that I was still in the Statistical Department.

Wonderful position! If relations with the Colonel became strained I merely had to suggest that perhaps I had better devote myself entirely to my real work. He was the ranking officer in

Berne, but I was responsible only to G. H. Q. . . .

For thrilling spy stories read Oppenheim or Buchan. The work of *contre espionnage* is not noisy. In France or England the general method was to spot a spy, censor his mail secretly, and, if possible, insert false information. To arrest and shoot him merely meant that he would be replaced by a new one, who in turn must be unearthed. In Switzerland, however, things were quite different. Anyone doing intelligence work, positive or negative, was liable to arrest. This made the censoring of letters, etc., impossible. There were two ways of doing business: either get all the dope on a German agent and pass it to a friendly Swiss *agent de sureté,* or, lure him near the French border, and Shanghai him across.

\* \* \* \* \* \*

Orders came through from G. H. Q., to try and convince the enemy that the American forces were going to attack in Alsace. The Colonel handed Howe and me the job. . . .

We met heavily, in the bar of the hotel. A fierce, low voiced discussion in a corner—business of scribbling, and comparing typewritten

## AND PEACE

notes. These were lists of pertinent questions as to roads, bridges, etc., in Alsace, implying an offensive in that region. By this time the barkeep was all ears, and interest. He even deigned to bring us our drinks, himself.

When we left, I gathered my papers together and buttoned them into my hip pocket, letting the important one slip out onto the seat behind me. Half an hour later, I rushed into the bar, hunted under the seat, in great agitation. Had I lost anything? Could the bartender help me? No, he hadn't seen any papers, and no one else had been in the bar. I assured him it wasn't really important. He smiled a slippery smile as I left, still agitated. One up to us.

Our next effort was a faked order,—carbon copy, signed true, and everything,—a beautiful piece of work. It took us a whole afternoon to make, and when we showed it to the Colonel, he tore around the room twirling his mustaches.

"Ha!! This means business at last! When did this come? Why wasn't it brought to me at once?"

Once more, we calmed him down, and explained.

We got in touch with a renegade German, in

his own territory, and after giving him a plausible story about being hard up, passed him the papers to show, and return. He may have suspected, but I heard he sold them for a good price.

We got tired of wasting time and energy chasing allied agents. With the English and Italians, we formed a central office, or clearing house, at Geneva. Marvelous! I grabbed the job of intelligence officer in command and became still more independent. Within a week, we found eleven authentic cases of shadowing our own men. Things began to pick up.

The second in command at Berne, let's call him Bernstein, got in touch with a renegade German—Zero. Then he got the grippe. He had a rendezvous with Zero the next day, but was too ill to go. No one knew Zero, and Zero only knew Bernstein. The connecting link was a post card, saying he would wait for him in the Station at Lucerne. Fine—at that time Lucerne was practically a German town. The Colonel gave me the post card and mumbled something about a message to Garcia—and that was that.

The station was full of interned Germans, in

## AND PEACE

and out of uniform. No use making myself conspicuous hunting for him here. I went straight to the hotel du Lac—Bernstein was a luxurious bloke—I felt sure he would have put up at the best. Half an hour later, allowing Zero plenty of time to walk back from the station, I sat in the garden along the quay. Any number of people were walking up and down. I watched to see which ones passed most frequently. One little German never seemed to be gone for long. I stepped under an arc light and studied the post card just as he was passing. Next trip, he passed closer, looked sharply at the card, and started whistling Tipperary. That was good enough for me. I followed him till we got to a dark place, then tapped him on the shoulder.

"Good evening, Zero."

"Where's Bernstein?"

"He couldn't come. Grippe."

"How do I know you're all right?"

"You don't. You've got to take a chance. I did."

We settled down to work. He talking, and I taking notes. We sat in the dark so I had to guide my pencil with a cigarette.

Next day, I shifted to a quiet hotel, slept during the day, and met Zero at night. This went on for several weeks; I reported at Berne at intervals.

Certainly Zero was in the inner ring. We passed his information to the Swiss police, who, thereupon, arrested Schreck, the head of German espionnage in that region. None of Schreck's underlings had a list of his agents, so they could not be warned. As they came to the surface, to find out what had gone wrong, the police netted them. The Germans searched furiously for the traitor. Zero and I had to be doubly careful.

Outside of Lucerne, there are two roads that run along the railway track—one each side. I met him, once, in the daytime on one of these, about a mile from town. We had hardly spoken when he saw German friends coming down the road towards us, in both directions. For a moment I thought we were caught. But luck still held—a long freight train was puffing down the track. Before the agents came near enough to recognize me, I had nipped across, and hidden by the passing train, got away on the other road. We kept to our nightly meetings, after that . . . .

## AND PEACE

Geneva was filled with deserters, professional spies, renegades, and dope fiends. The cream of the scum of the nations. I had been having difficulty with a suspect and the atmosphere was strained. "Nappy," one of our rough neck agents, took me aside one day.

"Look here. You've been having quite a lot of trouble with M——. Why bother with him? A hundred francs, and he goes in the lake to-night."

"No thanks, Nappy. I'm playing my own game, in my own way."

"Well, then, let us beat him up, so he won't get so fresh. That will cost two hundred, though, 'cause he might squeal, and there would be questions asked."

"Thank you, no!"

"All right! Have it your own way, but just let me tell you, if *you* don't, he *will*!"

* * * * * *

The armistice, a Bolshevik uprising, and the flu, hit Switzerland at the same time.

My official work was just beginning. Our prisoners in Germany had all been concentrated at Darmstadt. Some congenital idiot, in charge, sent all the officers by the first train; then for

## TEN THOUSAND SHALL FALL

seven days the men and non-coms arrived, a thousand at a time. It was a great game. I climbed aboard the train at Berne, at three in the afternoon, and took over. That was easy— I simply had the doors locked. But arriving at Geneva about eleven, I had to disentrain them, see that they were fed by the Red Cross, and hold them on the platform till the French train came in, about one or two in the morning. Then I must entrain them, check with the O. C. on the train, and catch the six o'clock back to Berne. The last night, I was met at Geneva with a flock of telegrams from Berne.

"Understand French train will not arrive tonight. Have men bivouac in station till further orders. Stop. Hold you responsible," etc.

Hold, hell! Seven hundred wild Indians just out of prison, and in a big town!

I don't yet know what I would have done, but I got in touch with Bellegarde, and found the train would only be three hours late. . . .

\* \* \* \* \* \*

January 15, 1919.
"Orders . . . . . . detailing the following named officers on temporary duty with the Peace Commission,

186.

## AND PEACE

Paris, France, are confirmed as having been necessary in the Military Service. . . . . . . . . . . . .
. . . . . . . . . . . . . . . .
. . . . . . . . . . . . . . . .

> By order of the Secretary of War.
> PEYTON C. MARCH,
> General Chief of Staff."

So we were to try a hand at Peace!

The Crillon was a glorious mixture of the University Club and the Eagle House at Concord with the State Legislature sitting, by heck! George left to perch on a heap of coal at Teschen, and I—Oh, I stayed on and helped arrange for bigger and better wars.

THE END

www.ingramcontent.com/pod-product-compliance
Lightning Source LLC
Chambersburg PA
CBHW060507090426
42735CB00011B/2137